FORTY YARNS
AND
A SONG

Barry Crump

**Moa
Beckett**

Books by Barry Crump

A Good Keen Man (1960)*
Hang on a Minute Mate (1961)*
One of Us (1962)*
There and Back (1963)*
Gulf (1964) – now titled *Crocodile Country**
Scrapwagon (1965)
The Odd Spot of Bother (1967)
No Reference Intended (1968)
A Good Keen Girl (1970)
Bastards I have Met (1971)
Fred (1972)
Shorty (1980)
Puha Road (1982)
The Adventures of Sam Cash (1985)
Wild Pork and Watercress (1986)*
Barry Crump's Bedtime Yarns (1988)
Bullock Creek (1989)*
The Life and Times of a Good Keen Man (1992)*
Gold and Greenstone (1993)*
Arty and the Fox (1994)*

* currently (1995) in print

BARRY CRUMP

Barry Crump wrote his first book, *A Good Keen Man,* in 1960. It became an immediate best seller, as did numerous other books which followed. His most famous and best-loved New Zealand character is Sam Cash, who features in *Hang on a Minute Mate,* Crump's second book. His first two books have sold over 400,000 copies and continue to sell at an amazing rate, some 30 years later. Two other Crump books feature Sam Cash, *One of Us* and *There and Back;* both are very entertaining and highly successful, and have been re-released due to popular demand.

Crump began his working life as a professional hunter, culling deer and pigs in some of the ruggedest country in New Zealand. After the runaway success of his first book, he pursued many diverse activities, including gold-mining, radio talkback, white-baiting, television presenting, crocodile shooting, acting and numerous others. His face is familiar to all New Zealanders through a series of motor-vehicle commercials which have won worldwide acclaim.

He is listed in *Who's Who in New Zealand* as author, of no fixed abode. He is currently somewhere in the South Island of New Zealand doing what he fondly calls research. He has contracted one of his books, *Wild Pork and Watercress,* to be made into a full-feature movie. In 1990 he wrote *The Life and Times of a Good Keen Man,* another book in the vivid style that has enthralled his readers for three decades. This is the author's own story, a fascinating account of the remarkable life of one of New Zealand's truly great characters. As to classifying his occupation, Crump insists that he always has been and always will be a Kiwi bushman, but perhaps these days 'itinerant scribe' would be more appropriate.

He was awarded the MBE in 1994 for services to literature.

FORTY YARNS AND A SONG
© Barry Crump 1994

Published in 1995 by Moa Beckett Publishers Limited
28 Poland Road, Glenfield
PO Box 100-749, North Shore Mail Centre, Auckland

Printed by Australian Print Group, Maryborough, Victoria, Australia

ISBN 1-86958-126-1

*This book is dedicated
to life in New Zealand
in the Fifties and Sixties.
Those great days!*

No reference intended to anyone in this book.

Author's note:

Esteemed Reader,

a brief note about this book.

A while back I wrote an autobiography called *The Life and Times of a Good Keen Man*. One memory evokes another and I ended up with a lot of material I couldn't fit in the book, things that have happened, things that have partly happened, and things that might have happened. The result of this is that some of these yarns are true, some are partly true, some aren't true at all, and some I'm not too sure about myself.

I present them for your entertainment. I hope you enjoy them and if I've captured some of the atmosphere of the times and they raise a chuckle in you I'll be well pleased.

Happy reading,

Aroha,

Crumpy.

FORTY YARNS
AND
A SONG

The Second of a Trilogy

CONTENTS

FORMATIVE YEARS

I WAS BORN in 1935 and one of my earliest memories is of lighting a fire when I was three. I found a box of matches and set fire to a bundle of hay. Under the house. Then I trotted round to the wash-house and told my mother to come and look at the nice fire. She didn't believe me until she saw the smoke pouring out from under the house. She believed me then.

There was much more fuss than I thought the occasion warranted. They put the fire out before it did any damage. My first fire. I probably remember it because of the spanking that went with it. It wasn't fair, either. The lady who owned the farm our father worked on had burnt a whole truck and load of hay just before that. They were trying to pour petrol into it in the dark and asked her to bring a light, so she went over to her house and came back with a candle and it set fire to the spilt petrol. Everything got burnt, but she didn't get spanked. They said that was an accident. Nothing's fair when you're a kid.

I survived and grew, despite repeated and determined efforts to poison me off. They had some rather strange notions about medical care in those days. At the slightest suspicion of worms I was force-fed two tablespoons of kerosene. Any sign of stomach-upset and out came the tall thin blue bottle of Castor Oil and my nose would be held while two tablespoons of the stuff was poured down my throat.

The average dose seemed to be always two tablespoons, which was a diabolical thing. You could usually make yourself swallow the first one if you were quick, but to get the second one down with the taste of the first one still in your mouth required reserves of courage you never knew you had. There was no pretending to be sick in the stomach at our place.

In those days there was a Rawleigh's man (never a woman), who came around all the houses with medicines and medical advice for the mothers. A modern-day Medicine Man. Us kids didn't like our Medicine Man any more than the African kids probably liked theirs, because after one of his visits we were usually in for a course of Milk of Magnesia (like drinking smelly chalk) to keep our stomachs healthy so we wouldn't need any Castor Oil, or daily doses of Cod Liver Oil (vile slime!) for our bowels, or (God save us) Black-Strap Molasses, to give us – of all things – iron!

At one stage our mother, bless her, inspired by an aunt who had no kids of her own to experiment on, lined us all up on Saturday mornings and gave us a revolting dose of sulphur and treacle "Because you need it. It's good for you".

Injuries, too, were treated with medieval callousness. Cuts and grazes were dabbed with a highly toxic chemical substance called Iodine that stung like wasps and far transcended any pain you might have been complaining about before that.

Burns were smeared with butter (or flour, according to the myth your parents subscribed to) and the burn was held as near to the fire as you could bear without screaming and then drawn away again very slowly. The reason given for this barbaric practice was that it drew the heat slowly from the wound and the butter (or flour) reduced the possibility of scars.

Bruises were handled in much the same kind of way. A poultice of some sticky kind of dough was applied to the bruised area at a temperature that had you just about clinging to the roof. Pain on top of pain! Prickles were gouged out of your foot with a darning needle: "Don't jerk like that or you'll prick yourself." Stoicism-building stuff.

11

Colds and 'flu were always treated the same in our house. If it was bad enough for you to stay away from school you were given a dose of the current poison to build you up and then made to sit hunched over a basin of crushed blue-gum leaves in boiling water with a towel over your head, breathing in the acrid fumes until you were almost fainting. Once again, the remedy was a worse experience than the ailment. We weren't sick very often at our place, we were too scared to be.

They had some funny ideas about food, too, when I was a kid. There'd been a war and rationing and the general attitude of the adult was that kids ate everything that was put in front of them, even things like marrow and cucumber, tripe and brains, tongues and livers. Anything that tasted good was bad for your teeth. White bread gave you soft white bones and brown bread gave you strong brown ones, and the crusts gave you curly hair, green vegetables gave you that iron we seemed to need so urgently, porridge stuck to your ribs, carrots gave you good eyesight so you could see in the dark, meat gave you a thing called protein which was so important that nobody could explain what it was, fat put a lining on your stomach, fish was brain food and improved your intelligence, eggs gave you energy and you couldn't eat too many of them, and fruit helped you fight off sickness. "An apple a day keeps the doctor away!"

In spite of the fact that most of the kids in our school lived on dairy farms, they made us drink a free pint bottle of milk at school every day because it gave us calcium, without which all our teeth and hair would fall out and our bones would turn to chalk. Whatever they told you to eat, you ate it, because it was good for you.

One of my brothers couldn't eat the fat off his meat, and if he didn't he didn't get any pudding, so he took to stashing his fat along a ledge under the big kauri kitchen table. He would have continued getting away with it except that he didn't get it out and give it to the dogs when no one was around, and his little subterfuge was discovered when our horrified mother, a meticulous woman, discovered maggots dropping onto the kitchen floor from under the table. I'll never forget poor brother Billy's face as he gulped down a big piece of mutton fat under the old man's watchful glare at dinner that night.

Our parents were fairly straight-laced and their statements about sex and reproduction were a source of constant amusement to us kids. Here we were on a farm, surrounded by things that bred – the dogs, the cats, the cows, the sheep, the horses, the chooks, the pigs, the rabbits in their burrows and the birds in the trees, breeding away all around us – and the old man tells our little sister that the bull jumps up on the cow so he can see over the paddocks.

Our mother was no better.

"Why is the dog pumping up the other dog Mummy?" our sister asked her one day.

Mum paused for a few moments and then said, "Because dogs go flat sometimes, dear."

No wonder our sister used to tell us other kids that she knew more about sex than Mummy and Daddy.

We all did, if they believed what they told us about it.

Apart from things like that, and all the work I had to do on the farm, and all the trouble I got into at school and at home, it was a happy enough childhood. I especially liked the farm animals and especially didn't like school. I was only barely average at school work, and I wouldn't have even been that if it wasn't for a rather strange set of circumstances.

Our parents and relatives and their friends subscribed to the "Children should be seen and not heard" school of thought and like all parents and relatives and their friends they didn't know that the kids knew more than the parents and relatives and their friends suspected. Our parents and relatives and their friends had a habit of spelling things out when they didn't want us kids to know what they were talking about.

"L-i-t-t-l-e p-i-g-s h-a-v-e b-i-g e-a-r-s," they'd spell out.

Being a nosy little brat I was determined to get to the bottom of this spelling business. I soaked up everything I could about words and what they meant and how they were spelt, and by the time I'd been at school for a year I could pick up enough of what the adults were spelling out to know what they were saying. And I heard some interesting stuff.

I found out that some people I'd stayed with had wanted to adopt me and my mother had been indignant about it. I knew who was going where for the holidays before any of the other kids. I knew when they were thinking about getting another car. I knew why the farmhand got kicked off Uncle Ned's farm so suddenly. I knew we were expecting another little brother or sister. They also spelt out a lot of stuff that us kids already knew.

This facility with words and spelling gave me a head start with that sort of thing at school and I'm sure that's what scraped me through the exams. I also scraped through that nightmare of contradictions they call childhood and emerged a semi-literate adolescent from the cocoon of family life, out into the wide world, still believing that you could get atomic radiation from sitting too close to a radio, heaven was up in the sky somewhere, hell was under the earth and yacht was pronounced yackt.

BUCKET AND SPADE

IN THE MITCHELLS' orchard, up a big pear tree. The ripest fruit is near the top of the tree and I'm high up in the branches, looking down on my brother. He's sitting in a nectarine tree, eating one and sticking one in his shirt. My shirt is already half full of pears. I climb higher to reach a ripe one and when I look down again my brother is scarpering through the orchard. He dives into the hole in the hedge and disappears. What's he up to?

I catch a movement out of the corner of my eye. Mr Mitchell comes down the rows of trees with a spade and a bucket. He stops and looks around and then comes and sets his bucket carefully down on a flat place and begins to dig a hole in the ground, right under the pear tree I'm perched in.

I hang there so still I don't even finish chewing the mouthful of pear I've just bitten off. I don't like the look of this. It's not just a bucket he's got, it's the full lavatory can.

For long minutes I cling there, looking down through the branches at the bald patch on Mr Mitchell's head bobbing up and down as he digs. My bare foot wedged in a fork of the tree is hurting but I dare not move.

Finally he sticks his spade into the ground and picks up the bucket and tips its contents into the hole and starts to shovel the earth back in.

Aghast at what I'm seeing I spit the pear out of my mouth into my hand and put it in my pocket. We'd been taught at school that what goes into the ground goes into the plant, and what

15

goes into the plant goes into the fruit. If Mr Mitchell puts that stuff under his trees it must be all through his fruit! I feel a bit sick.

Mr Mitchell steps back a couple of paces and looks up into the tree. I'm caught! I'll tell him I'm looking for our kite. I pretend to be searching for something higher in the branches, waiting for him to shout at me. He doesn't. I look down and he's walking away with his bucket and spade. He didn't see me!

As soon as he's out of sight I scramble down the tree and take to my scrapers, scattering pears out of my shirt as I run. I wriggle through the hole in the hedge and trot down the paddock and get through the fence into our place.

I catch up with my brother down by the Boggy Creek bridge. He's got some nectarines in his shirt and he's eating one of them, but he soon spits it out when I tell him what I've just seen and what he must be eating. We throw the rest of those big juicy nectarines into the raupo and cross the valley to raid the Rankins' turnips.

Mr Mitchell had done more to protect his fruit from the Crump boys with his bucket and spade than if he'd built an electrified fence around his orchard and patrolled it with guard dogs and Gurkhas.

ESCAPADE

I WAS ABOUT nine years old when this particular escapade happened. It was school holidays and our parents had gone out for the day. Us kids were to start the milking on our own that night if they weren't back in time.

My two brothers were eeling down in Boggy Creek and my sister and I were riding around on the school ponies. We got bored with that and started wheeling a big old tractor tyre from behind the shed around the paddock. It was a beaut thing, taller than me. We rolled it up the slope and let it roll down to see how far it would go before it fell over.

Then I got the idea that if we rolled this tyre right up the hill behind the house and let it go it would be quite a spectacle. It couldn't hit the house, even if it went that far, because there was a thick shelter-belt of macrocarpa trees in the way.

We rolled our tyre up past the house and through the gate and over to the bottom of the hill, and foot by foot we pushed and wrestled it up the slope. It was nearly too much for us and several times my sister wanted to give up, but I wouldn't let her. She was just about crying by the time we got the thing to the top of the hill and along to where it dropped off steepest.

We sat there for a while, getting our breath back, looking down on the house and sheds and the rest of the farm. We could see right out to the road but there was no sign of our brothers along Boggy Creek. They must have gone right up to the big pool where Leaning Tree Creek joined Boggy. I'd meant to wait until they could watch it, but I couldn't wait to see that tyre go down the hill, so we stood it up and rolled it over the edge and sent it on its way.

Now there was something I hadn't taken into account. Our neighbour had brought two hundred half-wild red cattle beasts down out of the bush up the back. The best way to get them to their place was through our place, and they'd got them as far as our swamp paddock and left them there for a couple of days to settle down and get used to fences. We'd been told not to go near them. They were feeding peacefully around down there below us like any other herd of cattle, and it was in their direction that our tyre wobbled off down the hill and began to gather momentum. It surely couldn't reach that far anyway, could it?

We watched fascinated as it gained speed and started bouncing as it hit the bumps in the uneven hillside. Halfway down it went sideways-on and looked as though it was going to trip up on us, but it flicked itself straight again and bounded on its way in huge leaps. It landed on the flat at the bottom of the hill from a jump that squashed it nearly flat and it sprang up into the air like something alive and bounded over the hill paddock towards the swamp paddock fence.

When the neighbour's cattle saw this big black thing leaping across the landscape towards them, they started running around with their tails in the air. The tyre hit the fence at the end of a bounce and flattened it and kept going. So did the cattle. They bolted in all directions and went through the fences in half a dozen different places and ended up scattered all over the farm. By the time the tyre wobbled to a stop and fell over in the bulrushes halfway across the swamp paddock it was the only thing left in the paddock.

What a mess! If the old man found out what I'd done I was going to be chain-harrowing paddocks for the rest of the holidays. With a combination of threats and promises I swore my sister to secrecy. We wheeled the tyre back and put it behind the shed and then went and found our brothers, and we discovered the confusion the stock was in when we came up from the creek to get the cows in. We didn't get much milk out of them that night because some of the neighbour's wild cattle got in amongst them and stirred them up.

The next day the neighbour and his boys rode over and it was concluded that something must have spooked their cattle. None of us kids had seen anything, we were all away eeling when it happened. They gave us a hand to fix up the fences and rounded up their cattle and took them over to their place.

I'd got away with that little escapade, but not completely. I was yet to find out what shameless little blackmailers young sisters can be when they've got an escapade on you. There were times when I would have preferred to have been caught red-handed. But that's another yarn.

THE KIWI BOMB

AH, THOSE WERE the days, when motor cars were new and most of us could only afford an old one. One of my earliest motoring memories is roaring up the Mad Mile at Takanini in our uncle's 1929 Dodge sedan, fuelled by a gas-producer burning ake-ake nuts, at a breakneck forty miles an hour. Awesome!

The motor car then was a very different thing from what it is today. They even smelt different: like cars. They smelt of leather and oil and dashboard, and if you owned a car you could never keep any decent clothes. As sure as you put on a white shirt you'd soon find yourself head-down under the bonnet, draining the carburettor bowl or putting the fan belt back on, and come up with grease and oil on you. You could't fill the grease cup on your water pump without getting a bit of grease on your hands. In fact you couldn't stand near a car motor in those days without getting oil and grease on you.

All the hoses were rubber and the containers were tin, no plastic in those days. Gaskets were cork or copper, and the petrol line was copper pipe with brass seats and fittings, always a bit cross-threaded. The wheels had split rims (a hell of a thing!), and if you could get 30,000 miles out of a car without having had to take the head off it to grind the valves or replace piston rings or bearings – well, you had 'one out of the box'.

One of our first cars when we were kids was a clapped-out Willys-Knight, a flash-looking thing. It must have been a bit embarrassing for the old man the day he brought it home after a win at the races, because I can remember him dragging the thing through the muddy gateway and up the hill to the house with our two draught-horses to show it to Mum and the kids. He had a lot of trouble with that car and ended up swapping it for a Whippet. That was the one we had before the Essex and then the Vauxhall.

A trip out in one of those cars was an event. When we were going somewhere there was rather more preparation of the vehicle required than there is today. One of the boys would pump up the tyre with the leaking valve, while the old man got under the car with a spanner and tightened the brake-rods. Then there was the check-list. The tool-box, spare tyres and the tyre-levers, tube-patching kit, pumps, mechanical jack and a couple of blocks of wood, tow rope, grease-gun, tin of water for the radiator, spare head-gasket, coil, cut-out and carburettor, and boots to put inside the tyres when they blew out. A spade and an axe were often necessary because of the state of the roads.

When all this was distributed in and around the vehicle, plus a bag of spuds and half a mutton for whoever we were attempting to visit, Mum and the kids would crowd in, Mum always in the front with the youngest of us. This was the big moment.

"Now don't you kids say anything," Mum would warn us. "We don't want to put him in a bad mood."

The old man would turn the key on, carefully set the choke and retard the spark and then pull her over compression with the crank-handle, careful to keep his thumb from round the handle because if she backfired it could break your wrist. Depending on the state of the car, cranking could be anything from a single lift on the handle to a frantic winding like you see them doing on those racing yachts.

When she finally fired, the old man would run round and do things with the choke and spark until she settled down running smoothly, then we'd all look round at each other grinning. We were really going!

The driving in those happy times was an experience all of its own. Country roads were always gravel and ours was two potholed wheel tracks with grass growing in the middle. We'd chug along at 25 mph, retarding the spark on the hills to get a bit more grunt out of her, and advancing it on the flat to save benzine, one and thruppence per Imperial gallon.

Passengers and driver were constantly alert for any change in the beat of the motor or the handling of the car. If she started missing it was probably a blocked main-jet or oiled-up plugs or dirty points, and if she started getting hard to keep on the road you were probably getting another flat tyre.

Cooling systems weren't as efficient as they are today and the radiators were very flimsy affairs. On long hills we often found ourselves parked up on the side of the road with a block or stone behind the wheel to stop her running backwards, the bonnet open and steam hissing out of the radiator and the smell of the rocker-cover gasket cooking. I'd be down in the gully with a tin looking for water, while brother Billy hunted around somebody's paddock looking for some horse dung to block the leak in the radiator with.

Some of those early cars had a thing called a vacuum-tank on them, a diabolical gadget that had something to do with the supply of petrol to the carburettor. They were always blocking up, sucking air, leaking, or just mysteriously failing to work. I didn't like vacuum-tanks because when ours packed a sad it was usually me who had to sit on the mudguard, wrapped in the old man's oilskin coat, holding up a gallon tin of petrol with the rubber hose off the windscreen-wiper siphoning into the carburettor. Siphoning petrol was such a common necessity I can still taste it.

Motor cars gradually became more sophisticated and less

understandable. The first electric indicators that came out were orange pointers that were supposed to come out of the doorpost and indicate which way you were going to turn. The only snag with those was that by the time we could afford to buy the car they were shot and hung half-out all the time, so it was back to indicating with your arm out the window. Electric windscreen-wipers were more of a success: they worked. You didn't have to let your foot off the accelerator to get the vacuum wipers to work any more.

Things like radios and cassette-players in cars were unheard of in those days, you couldn't have heard them without earphones anyway. And the only air-conditioning we had was a crocheted travel rug around our legs when it was cold and the windows open when it was hot.

But for all that those old cars had attributes that these modern jobs could never aspire to. For one thing they had running-boards, and you can't beat having running-boards. You could also take the spark plugs out of them and wind the car out of mud or a creek with the crank-handle.

As well as that you could pull up at the lake of any town that had one and lift your wooden floorboards and drop some bread under the car and grab yourself a duck or two for dinner. Try *that* in your Mitsubishi.

And you could fix them on the roadside. Many a Kiwi bomb has been kept on the go with wire or string or Mickey Mouse. I knew a fire-lookout bloke who got around in a Model A Ford for two years with two leather big-end bearings and the plug out of one of the other cylinders because the piston was grunted.

It's a long time since I lost track of the number of motorbikes and cars I've had. I once restored a B.S.A. 500cc single-banger bike, rode it for a while and then swapped it for a 1942 Ford truck with the twenty-one-stud flathead V8 in it, and restored that and swapped it for a partly-restored 1930 Model A Ford utility, finished it off and lived in it for three years.

No, you couldn't love or hate one of these modern cars like we loved and hated our cars in those days. You don't have to get to know them so intimately, and we've lost the sense of achievement on getting there, on having made it! But before you go shoving your Toyota over the bank, remember that it doesn't matter that you don't know what a gudgeon-pin is, you don't need to.

Today as I sizzle along the highway in my four-wheel-drive automatic wagon with the electric windows, sunroof, winch and mirrors, power steering and radar-detector, I don't give a thought to the possibility of a breakdown, and if one did happen I'd only have to pick up the phone and call up a service station to send out a car-fixing person. Tools and spares? I never carry them these days, I've forgotten how to open and close a crescent spanner.

No, when it comes to motor vehicles I don't think I'd like to go back to the good old days. I touch the button that changes the compact disc, flick her into cruise-control, adjust the air conditioning, and relax into the sheepskin. I'm cruising.

THE KIWI POSTBOX

Y OU CAN TELL a lot about someone by the box they put out at their front gate for the mail, and nothing expresses our ingenuity better than the good old Kiwi postbox. They can be as varied and individual as their makers, from immaculate miniatures of the house they serve, to something that's been slapped up temporarily until they can get round to building a decent one, never been painted, and years later it's still hanging together and doing the job. Other postboxes are made of concrete, brick or stonework, a welded 44-gallon drum, or carved out of a bluegum stump with a chainsaw.

The amount of care taken in the construction of a postbox tells us something of the constructor. Some postboxes are carefully designed and built to receive regular hand-written airmail letters from friends and family, while others have obviously been knocked up by people who never write letters and never receive anything but bills, bad news and brochures.

Some Kiwi postboxes are designed to take only letters, with maybe a tube for a rolled-up newspaper. Some are capable of holding the bread and the milk or perhaps a parcel or so. Then there's the country Rural Delivery box, big enough for the kids to take shelter in while they're waiting for the school bus, designed to take boxes of groceries, sacks of grain and a crate of beer for the shearers.

The Kiwi postbox is often adapted from materials found close to hand. They can be made from an old stove, a fridge, a vacuum cleaner, a petrol pump, a biscuit tin or a wooden barrel.

They can be an old cream can sitting up on a welded piece of chain, a plastic drench container nailed to a treated-pine post, or a gumboot set up on a stump. They all have a story to tell about the nature of the addressee.

They can be made of anything from steel to styrene, and shaped like a dog, a cat, a frog, a pig, an elephant or a pumpkin. There's a postbox near Nelson that's a replica of Parliament Buildings, with an axe embedded in it. And they can be set up on a crankshaft, a cream-separator stand, a plough, a fencing standard, a pipe, a post or a platform.

Standing alone on one leg or engulfed in the overgrown hedge, or in a cluster at the turn-off up a country road, the Kiwi postbox is usually equipped with a flag that can be raised to let the postie know there's mail in there to be posted.

Some people emblazon their names and numbers on their postboxes, some are discreetly printed so that you can only read them if you go and have a look, and some have nothing on them at all, which must be a hassle for the postie.

Many a student has helped pay his or her way through university by working as a postie, and enhancing their general education at the same time. At one part of it the late James K. Baxter, the great Kiwi poet, was our postie in a suburb of Wellington. Jim's round was so steep that the use of a bicycle was out of the question, he carried the mail in a big leather bag with a broad strap over his shoulder. Someone must have had it in for Jimmy because they kept posting bricks, thinly wrapped in brown paper and tied with string, stamped, and addressed to the last house up our street, the longest and steepest on Jim's round. Poor Jimmy must have carted twenty bricks up that hill, and the woman at the top had no idea who was sending them to her.

Jim never got along very well with dogs; they picked on him. He had a theory that dogs don't like posties because posties sneak up and put strange-smelling things on their territory and then, to add insult to injury, they blow their whistle. He panicked and threw his brick at a bulldog one day, and had no show of getting into the yard to retrieve it. I advised him to forget it or get another brick, and while he was still trying to decide on the best course of action the people with the bulldog handed the brick, with its tattered wrapping, in to the post office, and Jimmy had to cart it back up the hill. Such are the tribulations of the perambulating postie.

Dogs and bricks aren't the only hazards faced by the postie. They have to put up with wind and rain and sweltering heat. They have traffic, eccentrics and kids on bikes to contend with. They have to decipher our lousy handwriting and figure out which address is which and whose box is whose. They carry tons of junk mail and conscientiously attempt to deliver it, even if a pair of starlings, a possum or a swarm of Mason bees have taken up residence in your Thaibenzol drum. Unsung heroes!

A postie gets to know by the look of the postbox how easy or difficult it's going to be to get a registered letter signed. Some people are a bit chary of receiving registered mail, it's not always good news.

It was originally believed that the rigours of the job were such that only men were allowed to undertake it. Security was one important reason for this. In one instance I know of, two little kids followed a couple of hundred yards behind the postman with the tray of their tricycle filled with letters retrieved from people's postboxes. The little girl from next door and I had an impressive array of correspondence in our 'post office' in the hedge before we were caught.

Because she was only three and I was four, I got most of the blame. I was "thrashed to within an inch of my life!" by my grandfather, with a twig from a shrub in the yard with a little bunch of leaves on the end of it. I remember shouting some defiant thing at him about the lumps in his porridge in the mornings. Couldn't see what all the fuss was about, we were only trying to be posties.

That little girl from next door had to be the very first postlady in the country. A suffragette – while I was the suffrager. And now most of our posties are women. I feel quite proud of this contribution to women's lib – I trained the first one, and was martyred for it!

With the march of time and technology the postie and the postbox will inevitably fade off the Kiwi scene. The fax machine replaces the postlady with the brown legs, the parka, and the bag on her bike. We'll miss her like we missed the rattle of milk-bottles at the gate as we lay curled up in bed on a frosty morning.

So as you cruise New Zealand roads keep an eye peeled for that crazy Kiwi postbox, and spare a thought for the picturesque postie while they're both still around. There's a chuckle in it.

OLD BULLET

THE FIRST HORSE I had after I left home was a real good-looker. A thoroughbred race horse, a pacer, jet black with white fetlocks. He was a gelding and he could amble so fast that other horses had to trot to keep up with him. I paid five quid for him and I reckoned it was a real bargain for a horse as good-looking as that. I rode on a military saddle with a sheepskin over it, stock-whip coiled at the pommel, big hat, cowboy boots, two working dogs at heel – class!

Thus equipped I got a job on a sheep and cattle station, and one of the first jobs they gave me was to drove six hundred two-tooth wethers from a farm thirty miles away to our station. The boss took me in his truck and showed me where he'd arranged holding-paddocks and accommodation for me along the way. The next morning the boss pointed out a packhorse he reckoned I ought to take with me. It was getting a bit old and motheaten on it now but it had been used a lot for droving and was real handy. Its name was Bullet. So I caught Bullet and stuck a set of shoes on him and put a pack-saddle on him and loaded him up. It wasn't much of a load, sleeping bag, change of clothes, oilskin coat, a bit of lunch and a thermos of tea on one side, and dog chains, fencing pliers, some rope and some dog-tucker on the other. The boss also lent me a dog that he said would work for anyone, to beef up my dog-power a bit.

And so I set off on the thirty-mile ride to pick up the six hundred wethers, leading the packhorse and with the three dogs trotting along behind. The tattiness of the old packhorse and pack-saddle spoiled the effect a bit and leading the packhorse slowed me down considerably. He wouldn't hurry. It was after dark by the time I got there. I stuck my gear in the shearers' quarters, let the horses go, tied up the dogs, and fed them, and then went up to the house for a meal the farmer's wife had kept in the oven for me.

The next morning the farmer and I mustered the six hundred wethers and set me off on the road with them. I had only eight miles to go that day, to a station where my sheep were to be shorn.

Now there's a couple of things I haven't mentioned about that good-looking horse of mine. For one thing he was hard to catch, and if he got away from you he'd take off. He had a mouth like iron, and if you relaxed your grip on the reins he'd bolt. He was mad-headed, and skittery with traffic. Also I'd only had my two working-dogs for a couple of weeks and hadn't done any stock-work with them, so I didn't know what they were like. As well as that I'd never done any droving before. I didn't think any of this had been worth mentioning to the boss.

The first leg of the journey wasn't too bad, and by the time we got to the holding paddock at the station we were going to I'd learnt a few things about the horses and the dogs. Firstly, my good-looking horse was worse than useless. He kept crowding into the mob and I ended up walking and leading him all the way. My huntaway was hopeless and the dog the boss lent me was lazy, but he would speak up when I threatened him with a stick.

Old Bullet the packhorse was a real asset. He didn't need to be led, he just walked along behind the mob and never went past the last of the sheep. If Bullet stopped you'd know there was a sheep in the drain or up a driveway. Nothing would shift him until he had that sheep in front of him.

The following day the shearers shore my six hundred

30

wethers and the morning after that I set off on the next leg of my journey. That's when things started getting out of control. Without their heavy fleeces the sheep were as agile as dogs, diving through fences, dashing up driveways, jumping over drains. They were keeping me busy.

A mile from the station our route took us for about four miles along a main road. There was quite a bit of traffic and it scattered the sheep all over the place, and whenever I had to go and fish a sheep out of somewhere I had to find somewhere to tie my horse up first.

The dogs started getting lazy, I started losing my temper and the sheep did not cooperate. At one stage my heading-dog's head was sticking up out of a trough in someone's paddock, my huntaway was helpfully chasing a bunch of sheep through someone's garden, the borrowed dog was lying in the shade of a hedge, my good-looking horse was getting skittery, I was halfway up to my knees in mud in the bottom of a ditch, throwing sheep from between the bank of the ditch and the fence back onto the road side and a woman driver was calling out to me, "I say drover, would you do that again please? I wasn't watching."

We had to pass through a small settlement and by the time we were halfway through it I was ready to swear that everyone there had deliberately left their gates open and gone out for the day.

I was in a yard rounding a bunch of sheep out of a garden when I heard a loud BANG! And then another, and another. I ran to have a look. The pack-horse was kicking at the grill of a late-model car that had stopped behind him. As I approached the horse kicked the car again and there was a graunch and a squeal as the radiator went into the fan and water started pouring out onto the road.

There was a middle-aged couple in the car and the bloke got out and started bleating about the damage my horse had done to his car. Then his wife got out and said to him that she'd told him not to bump the horse with the car. He said it wouldn't get out of his way and I said that if he wanted to go around banging his car into the back legs of a horse he deserved to get it kicked in, and went back to my scattered sheep.

A couple of hours later, just before I turned the mob off the main road, the kicked-in car came past hanging off a break-down truck. I was walking beside Bullet at the time and gave him a pat.

It had been a hell of a day and darkness overtook me before I reached my scheduled holding paddock. I had to get the sheep off the road before dark so I went into a farm and asked them if I could put them in one of their paddocks for the night. They gave me somewhere to put my sheep, my horses, my dogs and myself and threw in a big feed and a bath, so the day ended on a better note. I sure slept well that night.

The next day I found a way to minimise the handicap my good-looking horse had turned out to be. I tied it short to Bullet's pack-saddle. It pulled back a bit at first but there was no budging Bullet. That left me free to walk behind the mob and retrieve stray sheep without having to worry about a skittery horse.

About five miles from home a truck came up behind us a bit fast and spooked my good-looking horse. It reared away from the truck and broke the leather strap I had it tied onto the pack-saddle with and came bolting through the sheep, scattering them in all directions. It galloped out of sight around the bend ahead. I gathered my sheep together and carried on. The horse would have to look after itself for the time being.

An hour or so later the boss arrived in his truck to see if I was all right. My good-looking horse had come galloping into the yard at the station. I assured him that I was getting along quite okay without the horse. I'd driven my six hundred wethers for twenty-five miles and ridden the horse for less than a mile of it. The last few miles were going to be even easier without the horse there at all. He'd been worse than useless.

Old Bullet, on the other hand, scruffy and tatty and old as he was, had taught me a valuable lesson. I got rid of the good-looking horse at the first opportunity and picked 'em on performance after that.

HANK

YOU GET TO know someone quickly and well when you live in a small hut with them and I've shared huts with some hard-case blokes. Most people stick to the rules and do their share of the cooking and gathering and cutting firewood and keeping the place reasonably tidy. Some blokes are fussy and meticulous and they can be a drag to live with. Others can be downright disgusting and such a one was Hank. I wouldn't put up with Hank for half an hour these days, but then I was young and still finding out about things. He could have been normal for all I knew at first.

I'd been laying fence lines with an HD5 tractor on a Lands and Survey block in Taranaki hill country and when that was finished the boss sent me to give the fencer a hand for a few days. He lived in a hut ten miles out from the station buildings, and he was the nearest thing to living with a scrofulous pig I ever had to endure.

They dropped me off at Hank's hut with some boxes of supplies, introduced us and left us to it. Hank was a wiry little bloke, a Dutchman, badly shaven, grubby and untidily dressed, with the dirtiest hands and fingernails I'd ever seen. His abode was a single man's hut, ten feet square, with two bunks in it, a table, a chair and a wood stove. I didn't notice the foul smell of the place at first because the hut was filled with smoke from the stove. He had the door open to let some of the smoke out. The mess was more obvious, it looked like a bomb had gone off in there. I couldn't find anywhere to put my pack down so I had to leave it outside until I found some space.

"Where do you want me to put the stuff off this bunk?" I asked him.

"Anywhere you like," he said.

That wasn't as easy as he made it sound. There was nowhere left to put anything, and among the stuff on the bunk was half a mutton carcass lying on a dirty sack. I found some wire and hung it up on the porch on a nail banged in for coats, put the bag of spuds and the pile of newspapers under the table and made room in the food cupboard for the bag of flour, the two cabbages and the tin of golden syrup.

"Where do you want me to put these clothes of yours, Hank?"

"Stick 'em anywhere," said Hank, who was poking around with the fire.

So I threw his malodorous shirt, coat, pants and socks onto his bunk. Then I turned my mattress over, had a look at it and turned it back again and put my stuff on it. My clean plate and mug looked out of place beside Hank's on the table.

"I've got a roast on," he said, poking into the oven with a sheath knife. "It's just about ready. Get some bread and butter out."

I found the bread and butter and put it on a fresh piece of newspaper on the table and began to cut and butter some slices. Hank stuck his knife into the sizzling hindquarter of mutton in the oven and lifted it out of the pan and carried it across and dumped it onto the table, dripping a trail of fat across the floor. Then he dug his fingers into a tin with salt in it and showered salt all over the meat, splattered tomato sauce over it from a bottle, carved off a layer of fat and meat, slapped it on a piece of bread and got stuck into it.

"Hook into it," he said, spitting out food through the gaps in his teeth as he spoke. "There's plenty there."

35

Somehow I wasn't hungry any more. Before I turned in that night I opened and ate a tin of spaghetti. We'd let the fire go out and the hut stank, among other things, of the kerosene Hank spilt when he filled the lamp. My mattress stank too, and Hank snored and ground his teeth in his sleep like a rusty door. I finally got to sleep by keeping my head inside my sleeping bag.

I was up early next morning, had a wash, split some wood and lit the fire. Hank got out of his bunk and had a leak and a hoik out the door, put his pants on and cut three sausages off a string of them and put them and three eggs in a frying pan on the stove with a big dollop of mutton fat. He threw the eggshells behind the stove.

Hank's method of washing his plate and eating-irons was to wipe them with newspaper and throw the paper in the fire. He did this and then forked the sausages and eggs out of the fat and put them on his plate.

"Yours is comin' up," he said. "We've only got one fryin' pan."

"I'll get it," I said quickly.

I cooked myself a feed with a bit less grease in it than Hank used and, breakfast over, we got ready to go out on the job. Hank prepared lunch. He threw the leg of cold mutton, the butter and a loaf of bread into a sack. At lunchtime I made myself a meat sandwich by cutting the outside off the meat, the bread and the butter and getting at something that hadn't been touched by Hank or the sack.

Despite his culinary shortcomings Hand was a good fencer and worker. We did ten chains of boundary fence a day and I learnt quite a lot about it from him. He was a bit ripe to get too close to. I mostly contrived to work at a safe distance from him, but it was almost impossible to get far enough away from him in the hut.

I couldn't eat any of Hank's cooking. He never washed and his food was usually drenched in fat. He got free mutton and made the most of it. I would have liked to clean up the hut but it was hard to know where to start. I found out why the stove smoked — it was choked up. I cleaned a big pile of soot and ashes out of it and it worked okay without smoking.

I scraped the fat off the table top, but then Hank cut up the chops and roasts on it with an axe and greased it up again. I scraped the floor of the hut with a spade and swept it, but within two days you couldn't see the difference. Hank had a habit of cutting firewood on the hearth and he knocked a pot of mutton stew off the stove with a piece of wood and spilt it all over the floor. He put as much of the meat and fat and cabbage and spud as he could pick up back in the pot, added more water and put it back on the stove.

When I asked him what he was going to do about all the stew left on the floor he thought about it for a moment and then suggested that we let it dry out and then just sweep it out the door. "If you're that keen to get rid of it," he added.

He would have been quite happy to walk around in it in his socks. I laid some sacks over it and opened myself a can of bully beef, but I couldn't eat it. The sight of Hank sitting on the edge of his bunk absently picking his nose and wiping his fingers on the leg of his pants was too much for me. I took the can of beef outside and ate it there, once I'd got my swallow back.

We were running low on bread and Hank decided to bake a loaf, but there was no way I could have eaten any of it. By the time he'd kneaded the dough it was a dark grey colour from his filthy hands. Added to the unappetising appearance and smell of him I was put right off my tucker.

If you live with a smell you usually get used to it after a while and don't notice it, but I could never get used to the kind of odours that surrounded Hank. He was fetid and reeking, and unconcerned about it. His bedding was a pile of mouldy grey blankets that stank something terrible. I was forced to ask him what the stink around his bunk was and he explained that a tin of neat's-foot oil had leaked into his blankets when he shifted out there. I suggested that he hang his blankets outside and give them an airing, but he just shrugged and said there was plenty of air in here. If it didn't worry him he didn't see why it should concern me. He was quite unaware that the air in the hut was so thick with the foul smell of his blankets that you could just about cut it with a knife.

We'd been told to come out to the station and have a bath or a shower any time, but when I suggested to Hank that we take half a day off and go out for a scrub-up he scoffed at the idea. It wasn't worth going all that way just for that. I asked him when he had a wash and he said sometimes, but I was willing to bet he couldn't remember the last time. He couldn't see the point in cleaning yourself up when you were just going to go out and get dirty again.

The worse it got, the worse it got, and by the time I'd been living with Hank for a week I was so disgusted by him I couldn't eat properly. Everything he'd touched was revolting to me. He was attracting rats and they were running all round the hut and keeping me awake at night, along with the stink and Hank's snoring and teeth-grinding.

I didn't last two weeks. I was becoming neurotic. I couldn't bear to touch anything Hank might have touched. If I couldn't smell him I imagined I could, and the faintest whiff of him made me nauseous. I felt unclean just from being this close to him.

I'd decided to throw the job in the following day, I couldn't stand any more of Hank, but the boss sent for me to do some tractor work out at the station and I gratefully left Hank in his horrific hut and went with the bloke who'd brought the message.

Couldn't get away from there quick enough and into a hot shower.

Since then I've run across a few codgers who've lived rough. They usually live alone and drift into letting themselves go a bit, but for sheer filthiness Hank the Dutchman was streets ahead of his nearest rival. If I hadn't met him I'd never have known how absolutely disgusting a bloke can get.

I know how smells can provoke memories and I know that memories aren't supposed to be able to provoke smells, but I could have sworn I caught a whiff of Hank just then. Must have been my imagination.

Unfortunate Experiences

O NE OF THE jobs I had in my youth was driving a
bulldozer for a drilling gang. About fifteen of us worked
for a contractor, drilling test-holes at the site of a
proposed dam on the banks of the Waikato River. We were a
good gang and getting the work done, a motley bunch from all
points of the compass, and one of us was a bloke called Joe
Zigfeld but he always got called Ziggy. He'd originated in
Austria and had spent a lot of time working on oil-exploration
rigs in Papua New Guinea and other places.

He was what you might call a bit of a swashbuckler, Ziggy.
Loved showing off. Flamboyant. Everyone liked him, especially
the girls. They thought he was cute, but then so is a leprechaun.
He was a professional rigger, which was an unlikely occupation
for someone like him. You see, he was a terribly unfortunate
bloke. Always coming undone in what he described as
"unfortunate experiences", and his description of it caught on
amongst us. Anything that went wrong was an unfortunate
experience.

There was quite a bit of humour in some of Ziggy's
unfortunate experiences. He was good at his job, and climbed
like a monkey, but whenever he tried his hand at anything else
it invariably ended up one of these unfortunate experiences.

For instance, there was the rope. Ziggy worked at the top
of one of the drilling rigs and he decided to string a rope from
the top of the rig to a stump outside the cookhouse, so he could
slide across on a pulley and not have to climb down from the

rig and walk around to the cookhouse, where he was usually last to arrive.

He got his rope rigged up and we gathered to see him try it out. He took a grip on a loop of rope he had on the pulley and, yodelling like Tarzan, he launched himself down the rope. Unfortunately Ziggy's rope was a bit slack and there was a steep gully full of gorse between the rig and the cookhouse. He ended up hanging in a big belly in the rope, fifteen feet above a mass of gorse bushes.

There was nothing we could do to help him. We couldn't even get to him. He dangled there stubbornly for a few minutes and then he had to let go. With a cry of despair he crashed down into the gorse. We cut our way through to him with slashers and brought him out. He was bruised and grazed and full of gorse prickles, dozens of them. An unfortunate experience.

Ziggy was off work for a couple of days over that but he didn't give up. He tightened his rope and retrieved his pulley and the next time he slid down he got quite a bit further across. He took a knotted rope with him this time and where he stopped he tied the knotted rope onto the main one and lowered himself to the ground, taking his pulley with him, then he crawled through the gorse up to the open ground. I bulldozed a track through the gorse for him to his landing point and everything went smoothly.

It was quite a performance. Every day at lunch-time and when we knocked off we'd all watch Ziggy launch himself down his rope and fly through the air, yodelling like Tarzan. He was now always first over to the cookhouse. But not for long. Ziggy was going to come undone again, through another unfortunate experience.

It had rained heavily the night before and it rained on and off all day. We were up to our ankles in mud. Just after afternoon smoko it began to look as though the rain was going to set in, and the foreman sent word around that we could all knock off for the day. We called up and told Ziggy, who gave his yodel and launched himself off the top of the rig on his rope. As usual we all paused to watch him and it was immediately obvious that something was wrong.

In those days before nylon all the rope was hemp, and hemp rope has certain attributes that need to be taken into consideration when you use it. It stretches, it tangles, it frays, it unravels and when it gets wet it shrinks and tightens up. And Ziggy's rope had tightened. It was as taut as a new fence. And he was going too fast. The yodelling stopped in mid-yodel as Ziggy realised the predicament he was in. He was never going to stop in time before he hit the knot where his ladder rope was tied on.

We watched fascinated as Ziggy hurtled down the rope towards that knot, kicking his legs in a hopeless effort to try and slow himself down, pushing in futile gestures at non-existent brakes.

When he hit the knot Ziggy made an unfortunate error of judgement. He tried to hang on, and as his momentum tore the loop of rope from his grip he flicked himself into a high arc that sent him flying through the air, still pumping desperately at those brakes as he plunged feet first into a big clump of gorse bushes.

We had to cut another track with slashers to get to him. He was lucky, the gorse had cushioned his fall, with prickles. He was bruised and grazed and had two broken fingers and a sprained ankle and hundreds of gorse prickles in him. He was off work for several days over that unfortunate experience and when he returned to work the boss told him to take his bloody rope down and leave it down.

But that wasn't the end of Ziggy's unfortunate experiences, far from it. We lived in two rows of single men's huts and on our way up to the cookhouse for dinner one night we called out to Ziggy as we passed his hut. He came to the door and said he was "doing something" and he'd come up shortly, but he didn't turn up for dinner at all, and as we went back past his hut we called out to see if he was all right. No reply. There was a sack hanging over his one window and his door was locked. We banged on the door and called out.

"Are you okay, Ziggy?"

We heard a strangled kind of groaning inside the hut. There was something wrong in there. One of the blokes broke the glass in the window and reached in and unlocked the door. The scene that confronted us inside Ziggy's hut is going to be hard to describe, but I'll give it a go.

Ziggy was a good-looking, well-built bloke, though a bit on the short side, which must have been bothering him because he'd answered one of those ads you used to see in the backs of magazines telling you to send your money and get a device by return mail, in plain wrapper, guaranteed to add inches to your height in just sixty days or your money refunded.

Ziggy's gadget had arrived and he'd set it up. It consisted of a harness that went around your head with a strap under your chin. A rope went from the top of this harness through a pulley attached to a hook that was screwed into a stud high up on the wall. Through the pulley the rope was spliced into two, with hand-grips on the ends. The idea was that you pulled down on the ropes and got stretched upwards by the harness on your head, thus adding inches to your height in just sixty days or your money refunded.

Ziggy had been pumping away there, adding inches to his height, when he lifted himself onto the tips of his toes and then tipped forward, hanging by his head with his arms locked stiff out behind him. If he'd let go the handles his face would have fallen straight into the pot-belly stove in the middle of the hut. He'd been hanging like that for some time and was in a bit of a bad way. He'd been having trouble breathing. We lifted him up and unharnessed him and put him on his bunk and got him a cup of tea. He came right but couldn't work next day because of a strained shoulder. Poor Ziggy copped a fair bit of ribbing over the unfortunate experience of the growing-tall gear.

Ziggy had barely recovered from the growing-tall gear when another unfortunate experience happened to him. We were sitting at breakfast one morning when there was a loud WHOOMPH!, an explosion, outside. We ran to the door of the cook-house to see Ziggy reeling away from one of our long-drop lavatories. His face was smudged with black and his hair and eyebrows burnt. He also had burns to one of his hands and arm. He was concussed as well. It must have been quite a blast in that confined space because the lavatory door was hanging by one hinge.

What had happened was this. It seems that Ziggy had a thing about spiders. We kept candles and boxes of matches in the lavatories and Ziggy was in the habit of striking a bunch of matches and running the flame around under the wooden seat, in case there were any spiders or wetas or anything there. Unfortunately someone had poured some chainsaw fuel down the lavatory to keep the smell down and the hole was full of petrol fumes. It had literally exploded in Ziggy's face. He was off work for nearly a week over that unfortunate experience.

Ziggy went from one unfortunate experience to another. He threw his washing into a drum half full of waste oil, instead of the washing drum. He bought a car and only had it for three days before it fell victim to an unfortunate experience. He tried to drive it through a slip that had come down in the rain. He got stuck and went off to get help, and while he was away more slip came down and carried Ziggy's car off the road and into the river. He never saw it again, there was a big flood on. No insurance. Most unfortunate.

Then there was Ziggy's girlfriend, a young lady who came round with an older bloke every now and again. Something to do with the unions. Her and Ziggy took a shine to one another and started going out. She lived with her parents in Hamilton and they were very well-off as far as we could gather. Unfortunately the romance didn't last long. Yes – you guessed it – more unfortunate experiences.

The first one was sheer bad luck. They were at the girlfriend's place all dressed up and getting ready to go out to some flash show, and the girlfriend's mother came into the room and caught Ziggy wiping some mud off his shoe on their living-room curtain. A small thing, really, but the old lady took grave offence and generated an unfortunate experience over it. She refused to have Ziggy in the house after that and he and his girlfriend had to make other arrangements.

They got in the habit of the girlfriend arriving in her Ford Prefect on Sunday mornings and taking Ziggy off for the day. This arrangement seemed to be working all right until one Sunday morning when yet another unfortunate experience overtook Ziggy. You might call this one a *very* unfortunate experience.

One of the blokes called out to Ziggy that his girlfriend was coming up the road. He emerged from his hut with a red and white bandanna tied around his forehead, a sleeveless denim jacket showing off his chest and the tattoo of a mermaid on his arm, gumboots rolled down at the top and the biggest belt bucket we'd seen. Thus attired, he swashbuckled down to open the gate for his girlfriend.

They both arrived at the gate at the same time, which turned out to be unfortunate because, although there was absolutely no need whatsoever to do so, Ziggy put one hand on the top rail of the gate and vaulted over it. Unfortunately the gate hadn't been latched at the other end and it swung open underneath him. He landed astride the top rail and then collapsed on the roadway in front of the girlfriend's car, gasping and groaning and rolling around clutching at himself.

I and another bloke who'd seen it happen ran down to see if he was all right. The girlfriend had got out of the car and stood there not knowing what do to. By this time Ziggy was crawling around the end of a tin shed at the gateway, into the gorse again. We followed him and asked him if he was okay.

"Get rid of her!" he croaked. "Get rid of her!"

So I went over and told the girlfriend that Ziggy was indisposed and would have to spend the rest of the day in bed.

"I think he's a bit embarrassed," I confided to her.

When she'd gone we got Ziggy to his feet and with us supporting him by an arm each he managed to totter up the rise to his hut, where he collapsed on his bunk doubled up and groaning.

Ziggy was off work for several days over that unfortunate experience and it also seemed to have had a detrimental effect on his relationship with the girlfriend. We never saw her again. Ziggy seemed to be more relieved than heartbroken over it.

"Those people are not like me," he explained.

There was a misleading spell of no unfortunate experiences for a while after that, and then the most unfortunate thing I could have imagined happened. A bunch of us went to a dance one Saturday night and ran into my sister and her girlfriend. And Ziggy and my sister fell for one another, head over heels! Within three months they were engaged to be married.

Now having someone like Ziggy as a workmate was one thing, having him as a brother-in-law was quite another. All those unfortunate experiences right in the family! A man has to be excused for feeling a certain amount of apprehension at such a prospect. I tried to warn the family about Ziggy's unfortunateness and they all stuck up for him. They wanted to know what I had against him.

"Nothing," I had to admit.

Despite the onset of a number of unfortunate experiences, some of them shared by my sister and other members of the family, the wedding plans went ahead. The day Ziggy was to become my brother-in-law drew closer. He was already beginning to treat me like one of the family. He even asked me if I'd be his best man, which I avoided by telling him it was against family tradition. I wasn't going to get too involved in any unfortunate experiences that were coming up if I could possibly avoid it.

You can call me a coward if you like but I didn't stick around for the wedding. Unfortunate experiences are a lot easier to take if you don't know they are going to happen.

Apart from the odd unfortunate experience, like Ziggy knocking a bloke off his bike on the way to the church and having to make a statement to the police and getting there an hour late, the marriage took place. Ziggy was family. My sister was Mrs Zigfeld.

Despite my justified misgivings, the Zigfelds moved into town where Ziggy got a job in the Fire Service, and they got on with living happily ever after. Ziggy's still with the Fire Service, quite high up I believe. They've paid off their house and raised three beaut Zigletts and they've still fallen for one another.

Notwithstanding all that, to this day whenever you see or hear news of Ziggy he's always just had some unfortunate experience or other, but we've got used to it. We wouldn't want him to change now anyway.

WOOLWORTH

I WAS ALWAYS keen on hunting, especially pig-hunting with dogs. When I was still at school I'd ride my bike fourteen miles over metal roads in the dark on Sunday mornings to meet an old pig-hunter who used to let me go hunting with him. He was one of the best pig-hunters around and other pig-hunters were always wanting pups from his dogs.

Old Sam preferred to hunt on his own and the only reason he let me come with him was because he was getting deaf and I had to tell him when and where the dogs were barking. Sam taught me things about the bush and hunting that stood me in good stead later on. We'd hunt through the bush all day and then I'd ride my bike fourteen miles home in the dark. I must have been keen all right.

For the first few years after I left home I knocked around the country, working on farms and driving trucks and tractors, logging, fencing, scrub-cutting, planting pines and so on, but whatever I was doing I was out hunting at every opportunity. By the time I was eighteen I'd hunted my way into a job shooting deer for the government in the summer and hunting pigs and goats in the winter. Suited me just fine.

In those early days of professional hunting in New Zealand the only training anyone got was none. They gave you a pack, a rifle and a sleeping bag and stuck you out on a deer-block. If you survived that and shot enough deer you had a job. If you didn't you were sacked.

Many of the blokes who took it on never should have. You

could tell within two days that they were never going to make the grade. They could be a terrible nuisance on a deer-block, and such a one was Woolworth.

We called him Woolworth because that's where he was working before he joined us, and Woolworths was all he could talk about. Within two days of the Field Officer dropping him off at the base camp my mate and I knew that Woolworth was never going to make deer-culling material. He was what you might call a dozy bastard. We couldn't let him cut firewood because we were on our last axe handle. We couldn't leave him in charge of the fire for fear he'd burn the hut down. He wouldn't go hunting on his own because he was scared of getting lost, and no one wanted to take him with them because he was too slow and too noisy.

We weren't too worried about him because the tally-book would tell the story and the Field Officer would take him back to town when he came with the next lot of supplies. Woolworth spent most of his time sitting around in the hut or going for short walks. He saw a deer on a fire-break one day but it "ran away".

My mate and I decided to go on a fly-camp for a few days and hunt a valley on the far side of the block. Woolworth didn't want to be left alone and after a bit of discussion my mate and I decided it was probably better to have him where we could keep an eye on him, so we showed him what to stick in his pack and let him come with us.

It was a five-hour walk to this valley we were going to but Woolworth slowed us down so bad it took us all day to get there. We had pup-tents with us but we didn't need them the first night because there was a dry cave we could camp in.

The only drawback with the cave was that it was full of cave wetas, hundreds of them. They're like a big brown grasshopper, three to four inches long. They jump like grasshoppers too. They won't hurt you but they take a bit of getting used to. They were under every stone and in every crevice in this cave. They came out at night and it was a bit disconcerting having them ticking on your sleeping bag or getting in your hair but when it's cold and raining outside you put up with that.

We dumped our packs at the mouth of the cave and I rolled a rock over to sit on and a couple of wetas jumped out. Woolworth gave a squeal and ran out of the cave and stood out in the open, flapping his wrists and looking anxious.

We started to tell him about the wetas being harmless but he interrupted us to explain that it didn't matter how harmless they were because he was arachnophobic. We'd never heard of it before but Woolworth insisted that it was a fair-dinkum disorder people suffer from. He was an arachnophobic, and arachnophobics have an unreasoning fear of spiders, scorpions, ticks and mites, and there's nothing they can do about it. What can you say when someone drops a yarn like that on you?

There was no way Woolworth was going back in that cave, so we erected a pup-tent on the bank of a little creek, thirty yards from the cave entrance. He made us make sure it was all pegged down tight. After we'd eaten Woolworth crawled into his tent and laced up the flaps and lit his candle and, as usual, read books half the night. That night he burnt a hole in the tent with his candle.

The next morning my mate and I were up before daylight. We wanted to catch the morning shoot on the river flats. We lit a candle and put our boots on. There were wetas everywhere. Hundreds of them. All over everything.

Woolworth had asked us to wake him up because he wanted to come with us. He still hadn't shot a deer and wanted to get at least one, just to be able to say he'd done it. So we decided to wake him up and fix his arach-whatever for him at the same time. I held the candle while my mate raked the tea billy around on the walls and roof of the cave and gathered up about fifty wetas. Holding a plate on the top of the billy to keep them in, we snuck down to Woolworth's tent with them. It was just getting light enough to see what we were doing. We untied the tent flaps and threw the wetas out of the billy into the tent and tied up the flaps again and snuck away and stood back to watch.

Nothing happened for maybe a couple of minutes, and then suddenly there was a blood-curdling scream and in one movement Woolworth burst out of his sleeping-bag and ripped the tent pegs out of the ground and threw the tent aside and ran screaming and yelling down the creek with no pants on, slapping frantically at himself. It was hard to believe that it was Woolworth who was yelling and running so vigorously. Not like him at all.

Well that was the end of our morning shoot. The deer would have heard that racket for a mile in every direction. We were a bit worried about Woolworth. He was sitting curled up on the bank a hundred yards down the creek. We might have sent him round the bend, he was a bit marginal at the best of times.

We made sure there were no wetas in his pants and took them over to where he was blubbering and sobbing on the bank. He wouldn't let anyone touch him but we managed to quieten him down and persuade him to stick his strides on. Then we lit a fire and had a brew of tea.

My mate and I had a yarn about what we ought to do. We had to get Woolworth away from that cave and it was no good taking him any further into the bush in the state he was in. The only thing to do was get him back to the base hut. So we stashed the supplies for later and shook the wetas out of everything and loaded up the packs. We had a bit of trouble getting Woolworth to put his pack on. He didn't want to touch anything. He was worse than ever at walking and it was dark by the time we got him back to the hut.

We'd thought that Woolworth might come right once we'd got him away from the weta cave, but he didn't. He was more distracted and vague than ever. He talked nonsense to himself all day and had a disconcerting habit of laughing in his sleep. We didn't like to leave him alone in that state so one of us had to hang around the camp all day to keep an eye on him while the other went hunting. This effectively cut our tallies in half. Woolworth was too dozy to even realise how unpopular he'd become.

It was hard to tell if Woolworth ever completely recovered from his traumatic experience with the cave wetas because it was hard to remember how dozy he was before that, but he seemed to be back to his normal degree of doziness by the time the Field Officer came and took him back to town. The Field Officer had crossed out Woolworth's name in the tally book and written – *Ceased duty. Not suited to this kind of work.*

Not suited! That was putting it pretty mildly, we thought. Woolworth had been on the block for six weeks. He'd been employed to shoot deer and he'd not only never fired a shot at one, he'd actually saved hundreds of them. As my mate observed, if Woolworth had got as many deer as he'd cost us he wouldn't have been a bad hunter. Definitely not suited to that kind of work.

BUSHMAN'S HOLIDAY

WHEN YOU LIVE in the bush for months at a stretch you naturally spend a lot of time thinking about what you're going to do when you hit the towns at the end of the season, but it never seems to work out how you dream about it.

I remember once four of us were dropped off in Taupo at the end of the season. There was Gutshot Grainger, Johnny Nailor, Hacker Hammond and me. We'd spent the previous eight months, from October to May, on deer blocks in the central North Island and we had two weeks to fill in before the winter season started.

We carried everything we owned with us, a rifle, a pack and the clothes we stood up in. Not really the right sort of equipment for a holiday in the Big Smoke, but it wasn't worth getting anything else for the short time we were going to be out of the bush. Now that we were here what were we going to do? That was always the big question. We stood around in a pub talking about life in the bush, and then we got the idea of going to visit each of our families and stay a few days and fill in the two weeks that way. Sounded a reasonable enough idea.

We went to Hacker's place first, in Napier. Hacker had warned us that his folk were 'a bit religious'. There was no sign that any of it had ever rubbed off on Hacker, and when we met his folks we realised why. They'd kept all the religion to themselves.

They were hospitable enough at first and didn't seem to

mind feeding us and letting us bunk down around the place, but after the first night they became introverted and withdrawn and spent most of the time in another room from us.

On the second day we were sitting around in their lounge, telling jokes and demolishing a crate of beer, when Hacker's old man came to the door and asked him if he could have a word with him. Hacker went out and had the word with him and came back embarrassed and told us we'd been asked to leave because our language was upsetting his old lady. We tried to square off but Gutshot put the lid on the whole performance by accidentally swearing while he was trying to apologise to Hacker's mum. She ran into her room and shut the door and we didn't see her again. We left on the bus the next morning.

Johnny Nailer's place was next on our list. His folks lived in Tauranga and when we got there we discovered they were millionaires or something. They lived in a big rambling house with a driveway and gardens and lawns. Johnny's old man was in the timber exporting business, and doing all right by the look of it. He was a friendly enough bloke and invited us into their huge lounge for a drink.

We cleaned him out of beer and then polished off some glass decanters of sherry and brandy and stuff. Before we knew it we were having a great old party. The only one who didn't join in was Johnny's stepmother. In fact she made it very plain that she didn't approve of 'this drinking'.

It was getting on in the evening. Johnny's old man and stepmother were out in the kitchen. The record we were playing stopped and we heard the stepmother saying, "You invited them to stay, you feed them. I'm not going to. They're disgusting. You can just get rid of them!"

It was Johnny's turn to be embarrassed. We all pretended everything was okay but it wasn't. We ate some bread and cheese and the old man showed us two rooms we could use, twin beds in each room. We didn't like to use their sheets so we got our sleeping bags out and slept in them on top of the beds.

But the day wasn't over. In the night Hacker, who was sharing a room with me, decided he needed to go to the toilet. He made his way up the passage in the dark to the front door and went outside, and the door swung to behind him and shut him out. He didn't want to wake anyone up so he went along the side of the house until he came to what he thought was the window of our bedroom. The window was partly open and he reached in and unlatched it and climbed into the room.

The sound of shouting along the passage woke the rest of us up. The old man had turned on the light and Hacker was standing in the middle of their bedroom.

"Oh my God!" shrieked the stepmother, clutching the sheet to her face. "He's got no pants on!"

Gutshot and Johnny and I reached their bedroom door just as Hacker came scuttling out holding his shirt-tails down at the front and back. We got the story off him and tried to explain what had happened to the stepmother but she wouldn't be consoled, in fact she got hysterical whenever one of us said anything to her. In the end the old man said we'd all better go back to bed. So we did.

The next morning Johnny's old man cracked it for a chat with him out on the lawn and the upshot of it was that we were back on the bus that afternoon, heading for Gutshot's folks' place. They had a farm a few miles out of Thames and sounded more like our kind of people.

We got a ride out to the farm on a milk tanker. It was a typical cockie's outfit. Old farmhouse, sheds, herd of cows in the paddock, chooks and ducks running around. We were looking forward to getting along a lot better with Gutshot's folks as we walked up the long muddy driveway, but it wasn't to be.

Gutshot's family turned out to be in something of a turmoil.

His old man was sitting in the kitchen mumbling drunk on home brew beer. He didn't seem to be particularly overjoyed to see us. He mumbled on about some trouble he'd been having with the family. From what we could gather Gutshot's old lady had run away with the Noxious Weeds Inspector, his older brother was in jail for burgling some shops, his sister had been sent out of the district in disgrace for some shenanigans she'd been up to with a married man, and Gutshot's young brother had just been suspended from the High School for being caught smoking. The old man had a bunch of his friends coming out from the pub that night to help him celebrate.

Four carloads of them turned up, all well on the way when they arrived, and a hooley got under way that lasted until after dawn the next day. They had two guitars with them and they arrived singing. We tried to join in but they all had a head start on us and we never got into their mood.

A Maori sheila took a shine to Hacker and ended up sitting on his lap. Hacker didn't seem to mind in the least but her husband was taking a pretty grim view of it. He was glaring at Hacker with a look that meant trouble was coming up real soon, but Hacker was oblivious to it. Johnny and Gutshot and I got Hacker outside and told him why we'd decided not to intrude on these good folk any longer. We took our packs over to Gutshot's old man's hayshed and slept there in the hay, whenever the noise from the house allowed.

Our slumbers were disturbed by a drawn-out argument about someone wanting to drive off in a car and someone else not wanting them to. A fight started but didn't come to anything except noise. The guitars and singing thumped on through the night.

Some time in the early hours of the morning a couple sneaked into the hayshed and started necking in the hay not six feet away from me. Their giggling and whispering woke me

56

up. They obviously had no idea we were there. The woman seemed a bit nervous and reluctant and the bloke was trying to talk her into it. When I'd figured out what was happening I suddenly let out a loud scream,

"AAAAGH!"

Johnny and Hacker and Gutshot sat up in the dark from where they were lying in the hay, demanding to know what the hell was going on.

"Yeah, what's going on?" I echoed.

As long as those two people live I know they won't forget that. The bloke got such a fright he abandoned the woman he'd been so ardently chatting up and bolted for the door, stumbling and grunting in a blind panic. We found one of his shoes stuck in the mud in the gateway next day. The woman tried to follow the bloke and stumbled into Gutshot in the dark and fell across him, screaming her head off. We saw her silhouette as she scrambled out the door on her hands and knees. It was going to be a while before anyone was going to lure her into a dark shed again.

We had a good laugh over that and when we settled down to try and sleep again Gutshot got all embarrassed.

"Sorry about all this, you guys," he said in the dark.

"Don't worry about it, Gutshot," we told him. "It could've happened to anybody."

In the morning we went over to the house and looked around at the bodies lying asleep everywhere, the bleary survivors, the bottles and flagons, the spilt booze and overflowing ashtrays. The bleary survivors were trying to organise someone to go and get another keg of beer. We weighed up the situation and came to the conclusion that we weren't going to be much use around here. Gutshot left a note for his old man, who was snoring in his chair, and we got a lift into Thames with a bloke who'd had some sleep.

We had a feed in Thames and then got on a bus to Auckland, to visit my folks. We'd planned to fill in two weeks at the four places and we'd gone through three of them in four days. It wouldn't be like that at our place though. My folks were good sorts, especially my mum. She'd be blown away to see us, I could guarantee that.

Our house was in a residential suburb and it was about ten o'clock at night when we arrived there in a taxi from the bus depot. My folks were out, there was no car in the garage, but that didn't matter. Nobody locked their houses in those days. We dumped our packs in the lounge and raided the fridge and had a big scoff-up of cold chicken, salad, luncheon, cheese and slabs of bread, washed down with a few bottles of my old man's beer. Then we took it in turns to have a bath.

By half past twelve they still hadn't come home so we got into our sleeping bags on the lounge couch and floor and yarned for a while and it wasn't long before we were asleep. We hadn't got much sleep in Gutshot's old man's hayshed the night before.

When I woke up the next morning there were voices in another part of the house. I heard my old man call out, "Who the hell's been in this bloody bathroom?"

Johnny's sleeping bag had several holes in it patched with sticking plaster and one of them had come apart in the night and there were feathers all around him on the carpet but Mum wouldn't mind that.

I woke the others to watch what happened when my folks found we were there. We sat up in our sleeping bags and waited. Footsteps came up the hallway and the door opened and my mother walked into the room in a petticoat, only I'd never seen her in my life before.

At first the others didn't know there was anything wrong. The woman looked around at us and then yelled out, "Bob!" and ran out of the room and up the passage yelling,

"Bob! There's a whole lot of men in the living room!"

The others were looking at me. It was my turn to be embarrassed.

"What's wrong?" said Gutshot.

"That's not my mother," I said.

"Then who is it?" said Johnny.

"I don't know," I said. "I've never seen her before."

"Who's Bob?" said Johnny.

"Not my old man, anyway," I said.

"Oh hell," said Hacker. "Not again."

"I'm afraid it looks a bit like it," I said.

Bob appeared in the doorway and to give him credit he handled the situation quite well under the circumstances. Four bushrats had bowled into his house and eaten his food and used his bathroom and made a hell of a mess and camped in his lounge and filled the place with feathers. He looked around at us and our packs and rifles and then said, "Who are you?"

I told him my name and asked where my folks had moved to. He'd never heard of them. He'd bought the place two years before through an agent. I was able to prove I knew the house, I'd lived in it for two years. My folks must have sold up and shifted more than two years earlier. I hadn't realised I'd been out of touch that long.

The people were pretty decent about it once they'd realised a genuine mistake had been made and wouldn't take any money for the food or the feathers. They just wanted us to go. So we were out on the suburban footpath with our rifles and packs and people hurrying to work all around us. Not our sort of country, we were definitely out of place here.

We waved down a taxi and went to the bus depot and bought tickets on the next bus going south. That night we cleaned up an old rabbiter's hut on the shore of Lake Taupo and moved into it to wait out the other week in comparative calm, until the season started and we could go back into the bush where we belonged, with enough yarns about our adventures in the towns to last all season.

We used to sit round our fires at night and wonder how the people who lived in the towns could keep that sort of thing up. In the bush we often went for weeks without sleeping in the same place twice and thought nothing of it, but in the towns a week of it was all we could handle.

Life sure was complicated out there.

SENSE OF HUMOUR

I'D FINISHED A summer deer season in the Kaimanawa Ranges and there was a month to fill in this time before we got our winter hunting blocks, so I moved into a flat in Grafton in Auckland with a bloke I'd met in the bush and got a job in the woolstores. A drastic change of environment. It was hard, monotonous work but the money was good and it was only for a short time.

My workmates were a motley bunch and one of them was a little joker called Johnny who had a real hard-case sense of humour. He pulled some pretty outrageous stunts and got away with them, mainly because he was so innocent-looking and straight-faced about everything. He was a likeable enough bloke and brightened many a smoko with his off-beat way of looking at things. You had to watch him in case he pulled one of his capers on you, but no matter how closely you watched him, Johnny would get you if he wanted to.

One of the blokes who had known him on another job reckoned that Johnny swiped a roll of toilet paper one wet night and laid it up the middle of the road, continuing the white line around a bend and swerving it all over the road, causing a great deal of confusion among the traffic and a couple of near accidents.

Just after I started at the woolstore Johnny stuffed a pair of jeans with wool, put a pair of gumboots on the end of the legs and pulled a four-hundred-pound bale of wool off a stack onto them, leaving the pants and boots sticking out from underneath it.

Someone found it there and raised the alarm and the whole outfit came to a shocked standstill. We all thought someone had been killed. When we lifted the bale of wool away and found nothing but wool in the pants we all turned to Johnny, who was sitting there expressionlessly rolling a smoke. There was no doubt who'd done it. The foreman told him that if he did anything like that again he was down the road. Johnny grinned and agreed with him and we were all told to get back to work.

Looking back, it's a wonder someone didn't clock him one, but it didn't happen while I knew him. It would have been kind of admitting you couldn't take a joke.

We used to have lunch in a pub at the bottom of Queen Street and we were just leaving there one day when Johnny struck again. He politely held the door open for one of the blokes and as he went through it Johnny suddenly grabbed him by the back of the collar and the seat of the pants and ran him across the footpath outside, bumping aside several pedestrians, and threw him into the gutter.

"Don't you come in here behaving like that!" he shouted at our bewildered workmate. "If you ever do anything like that in here again you'll be barred for three years!"

The poor bloke could only pick himself up and slink away, pursued by the curious stares of the two dozen or so people who'd witnessed his ignominious expulsion from the pub. The rest of us just couldn't help laughing.

He got me one day. He and I had been sent to help out at another woolstore a few hundred yards around the waterfront. There were quite a few pedestrians at the time and something about the way they were looking at us made me look around at Johnny. He was striding manfully along beside me with a clubbed foot and his shining bale-hook sticking out the sleeve of his jacket.

"Cut it out, Johnny," I said to him. "What the hell

do you think you're doing? People are staring at us."

"I'm only trying to keep up," he said loudly and plaintively. "You're going too fast for me."

I had no reply to that, so I quickened my pace until I was trotting through the oncoming pedestrians. Johnny pursued me in his grotesque gait.

"Please, Crumpy!" he called out, groping towards me with his hook. "I can't keep up. You're leaving me behind!"

Everyone we passed stopped and looked around at the heartless swine who was treating that poor handicapped chap like that. He kept it up all the way to the woolstore we were going to. I dived gratefully off the street in through the doorway. Johnny strolled in after me, jauntily swinging his bale-hook. I could have throttled him, but what can a bloke do? He'd got me one.

But I'd got off lightly. One of the other blokes was walking along a crowded street with Johnny one day not long after that, when Johnny suddenly jumped aside from him and shouted, "How dare you touch me like that! You just keep your filthy homosexual hands to yourself! If you ever do that again I'm calling the police!"

The poor bloke could only stand in front of the gathering crowd, groping for words.

"I didn't touch him," he protested.

"You know damn well what you did," shouted Johnny, "and if you ever do anything like that to me again I'll get the police onto you! Now get away from me, you filthy beast!"

The poor bloke was highly hacked off when he arrived at work and told us what Johnny had done to him.

"What did you do?" someone asked him.

"I ran," said the bloke. "I'll murder that bloody Johnny if he ever does that again."

I knew how he felt.

A bit later Johnny sauntered in and made some witty remark that got us all laughing, and he'd got away with it again.

Johnny's next victim was a young bloke who'd just started working there. It was his first job. He'd got the morning off to go to the dentist and we'd told him to meet us at our usual pub for lunch. He was there when we arrived. Johnny went straight up to him and said, just loudly enough for the other people in the bar to hear him, "My word, young feller. You can thank your lucky stars this time, but you won't get away with anything like that again."

The whole bar went quiet.

"Like what?" stammered the young bloke.

"Now it won't do you any good to go playing the injured innocent," said Johnny sternly. "You know jolly well what. Now the police are prepared not to press charges unless the girl's parents insist. You're just lucky she's not pregnant!"

"But I've never done anything like that to her," said the flustered young bloke. "We only kiss a bit and that. Who told you . . . ?"

"Never mind who told us," said Johnny. "But it's a very serious offence doing that sort of thing to an under-aged girl. The best thing you can do at this stage is go and apologise to her parents and promise you won't do anything like that again."

The young bloke gaped blushing around at the audience.

"I – I thought she was seventeen. It only ever happened the once, you know," he mumbled.

"Well just you make sure it doesn't happen again," warned Johnny, picking up his beer and shaking his head at the enormity of the young bloke's misdemeanours.

Later on a couple of blokes bailed up the young bloke and explained that Johnny had only been having him on. He must have been greatly relieved.

Looking back on some of these pranks it's difficult to

believe we found them as funny as we did, but we did. People's sense of humour apparently changes with the times.

Johnny went on playing his tricks. He got me once more. A fresh egg substituted for a hard-boiled one in my lunch. One day he fitted one workmate's car between a power pole and the side of the building. There were about three inches to spare at each end of the car and we had a hell of a job getting it out. It was only later that we'd found out how he'd put it there. He'd used one of the forklifts.

A few days before I left there and headed for the tall timber in the Ikawhenua Johnny finally pulled a stunt that backfired on him. Our foreman picked out four of us to go across town with him to load a truck with bales of wool that had been temporarily stored in an old warehouse. We caught a Council bus outside the woolstore. Johnny sat up the front of the bus beside the foreman, who had been described by one of the blokes (a university student) as, "a man of singularly humourless disposition."

Partway through the journey the bus was stopped at an intersection and Johnny suddenly said to the foreman in a loud voice, "Now don't forget what the doctor said, any more of that behaviour like last time and you won't be allowed out at all!"

"What the hell are you talkin' about?" said the foreman.

"Now you know you mental patients are only allowed on these excursions provided you behave yourselves," said Johnny seriously. "And after that disgraceful behaviour of yours last time you're on your last chance."

"Behaviour!" roared the foreman. "I'll give you behaviour, you cheeky little bastard! You're down the bloody road. You can go back and pick up your time!" The bus pulled over to the kerb and stopped and the driver said, "I'll have to ask you two to get off the bus. We don't tolerate this sort of thing on the buses."

"It's this bastard here," said the foreman indignantly.

"Off you get, both of you," said the driver. "If you don't get off this bus immediately we're going straight round to the police station."

So Johnny and the foreman had to get out and the bus drove away, leaving them arguing on the footpath.

The other three of us had been trying not to laugh too loud, but we stopped laughing when we realised that none of us knew where we were supposed to be going. We got off a few stops later and waited more than half an hour for a bus that would take us back to the woolstore. As we approached the woolstore we spotted Johnny walking along with his bag. Down the road. Finally a victim of his own sense of humour.

I used to think it'd be interesting to follow Johnny around just to see what he got up to, but he'd have been a hard act to follow round. No, it doesn't pay to get to know the Johnnys of this world too well. They can be good value but they do need spreading thinly.

THREE DOG NIGHT

IN THE DAYS when I was young and knew everything, I was living and working in the Urewera country, two million acres of native bush in the central North Island. In the winter we sometimes trapped possums for skins, waiting for the next deer season. We knew the bush like the proverbial backs of our hands.

A mate of mine and I had spent three days scraping and brushing several hundred possum skins we'd trapped in the Waiau Valley and I was taking them into town in our fifteen-hundredweight Bedford with a canvas canopy on the back.

Around the shores of Lake Waikaremoana there was a small clearing on the top of a big ridge where the cattle drovers used to have a holding paddock in the old days. There weren't many wild pigs in that area but a small mob of them lived around that ferny clearing and at the time I had three pretty good hunting dogs, even if I do say so myself. I decided to have a go at taking some wild pork into town for a mate of ours who couldn't get out hunting any more. The dogs had been on the chain for a few days and a run would be good for them, even if we didn't get anything.

I pulled up at the side of the road and let the dogs out. It was late afternoon and the wind was right and before we'd got the three hundred yards along the ridge to the clearing the dogs winded something and shot away and knocked up a pig. Before I could get there it had chucked off the dogs and bolted away down into a steep dirty creek-head and before they could stop it they were halfway down to the river on the other side of the ridge. I could tell by the footmarks in some fresh rooting that it was a hefty boar.

I scrambled after them and when I got there two of the dogs had the pig by an ear each and the other one was barking to let me know where they were. It was a big young boar, about a hundred and thirty pounds weight and in good condition. A good eating pig. I stuck it and gutted it and carted it on my back out onto a leading spur and began the long climb back up to the top of the ridge.

By the time I'd made it to the top it was getting dark and starting to rain, and by my reckoning I was still a good half hour from the road. It got darker and wetter and pretty soon I couldn't see where I was going. All I could do was fumble my way through the bush, careful not to lose any altitude, and hope I could come out on the road. I was fairly sure I'd missed the little clearing but the road had to be somewhere in the direction I was heading.

After about an hour of stumbling and tripping and banging into trees and getting caught up in vines I had to admit I was bushed. I wasn't even sure I was going in the right direction any more. It was pitch dark and I was disoriented. I dropped the pig and got into the bole of a big rata tree and huddled there and settled down to wait out the longest of nights, soaking wet, wind blowing, rain pouring down, tobacco and matches left on the seat of the truck, and crawling with pig lice. Pig lice don't bite you but they sure do crawl. I hadn't laced up the canvas flap on the back of the truck and our possum skins were probably getting wet, but that was the least of my worries.

Hour after hour I sat it out. The only warmth I had was the dogs and they kept sneaking away and had to be whistled back so I could cuddle into them. A three dog night!

It's hard to describe how long these nights are, aware of every minute and realising how many more of them you have to endure. It's endless. No thought can divert you from the discomfort. Getting up every now and again to jump up and down to ease cramped limbs and get a bit of circulation going. Scratching, shivering, talking to yourself and anyone else you can think of, starving hungry, thinking of your mates curled up cosy in their warm sleeping bags enjoying the sound of the rain on the roof of the hut and the wind whistling in the chimney, watching for the lightening of the sky, no idea what the time really is. I had a watch on but I couldn't read it.

Before that and since then I've spent a few uncomfortable nights. One I won't forget is the time I waited out the night wrapped in a ripped river raft. That was pretty clammy. Another time I sat it out wrapped in green deer skins at four and a half thousand feet in slushy snow on the Kaweka Range. Then there was the night another bloke and I spent the whole night in a hot pool at Atiamuri and by morning we were so weak from dehydration we had to help each other walk a hundred yards in flat going out to the road, like a pair of drunks.

Another time a mate and I were jet-boating the Motu River and decided to retrieve a billygoat we'd shot for dog tucker. It was hung up in a koromiko bush on a steep rock face above the river. My mate held the nose of the jet-boat against the rocks while I climbed up and got the goat. I gutted it and threw the guts into the river upstream of the boat and they got sucked into the intake, instantly cutting off all power. I watched my mate carried helplessly away down the river and out of sight around the bend. He hadn't come back for me by dark and I had to spend the night wedged between a small tree and the rock face. They came and got me the next day.

They're long nights, those ones, but this was the longest and most uncomfortable in my memory. I sat there with a dog under each arm and another between my legs until the sky really did begin to fade into the grey light of dawn. I waited until it got light enough to be able to move through the bush. Then it had the effrontery to stop raining.

I stood up and stretched and looked around, trying to figure out my direction. The dogs trotted off and I looked in the direction they took and there, not fifteen yards above me, I saw the wheels of the truck parked at the roadside.

How embarrassing for a bushman who knew everything! The dogs must have thought I'd gone completely mad. All night they'd been trying to sneak away to keep dry under the truck, even if I did choose to sit out in the rain.

Not one vehicle had come along the road all night, and just as I dragged my pig up onto the road the venison truck came along and stopped when they saw me. The driver wound down his window and said,

"Spare me days, Crumpy. You're a bit keen aren't you mate! Good pig eh!"

"Ar, you've got to get up early if you want to get a bit of pork around here," I said.

Sitting all night in the rain fifteen yards away from your truck is something a professional bushman prefers to keep to himself. I'd appreciate it if you didn't tell any of my mates about this. And anyway, because of that and a number of other humiliating experiences that have overtaken me in the intervening years I no longer claim to know everything.

GUTS

A<small>T ONE STAGE</small> of it I was living in a shack at the foot of Mt Tauhara, working for the Taupo Rabbit Board. It was mostly dog-and-gun work and we were using a hundred shotgun cartridges each every day. There were a lot of rabbits around there.

After work one afternoon I stopped for a beer at the old Terraces Hotel on my way home. I noticed three Maori blokes come into the pub. I didn't know them. The toilet was outside the bar and when I went to use it I saw Digby Hollister's pig-dog, Mack, on the back of the Maori blokes' truck parked near my ute. I knew the dog well. It was a quarter-bull, black and white with a big white spot on one side of him with a pig-rip scar through it. I'd been using him when he'd got that rip. Digby would never have parted with him, he was his best dog.

Those Maoris were inclined to swipe the odd pig-dog. They'd pinch them and send them to their cousies in another district. Well, we'd see about that.

I had a bit of trouble getting Mack off their truck. They must have had him for a while because he didn't recognise me. I had to get a chain off my ute and put it on him and drag him off their truck. I was dragging him across to my ute when one of the Maori blokes came out of the bar.

"Hey boy! What are you doing with our dog?" he said.

"Like hell it's yours," I said. "This dog belongs to a mate of mine from Ngongotaha."

"That's our dog, boy," repeated the Maori bloke, and he went back into the bar.

I got the dog by the scruff and threw him onto my ute, where he immediately got into a fight with my black-lab retriever. By the time I'd dragged him off the back and shoved him into the cab and shut the door on him the three Maori blokes had come out of the bar.

"What are you doing with our dog boy?" said one of them.

"This dog belongs to Digby Hollister from Ngongotaha," I said, "and he's going back."

"No boy, it belongs to our cousin. He lent it to us."

"Pull the other one," I said. "I've known this dog since it was a pup, and it's going back to its owner."

A few other blokes had come out of the bar to see what was going on. The three Maori blokes mumbled among themselves and then wandered back into the bar. I got into my ute and roared off. That had been easier than I might have expected.

Having done my good deed for the day I couldn't wait to be patted on the head for it. I stopped at a neighbour's farm where they had the phone on and looked up the number and rang Digby in Ngongotaha. His wife answered the phone and called him in from outside.

"I've got Mack here, Digby," I told him. "Some Maoris had him on their truck at the Terraces pub."

"What the hell are you talking about?" he said. "Mack's tied up outside. I've just fed him."

I suddenly realised that I'd made a very naughty mistake. Of course that wasn't Mack out there in the ute. It didn't even look the same, come to think of it, and it certainly didn't behave like Mack. I'd pinched a dog off those Maoris.

I got in the ute and shot back to the pub to try to catch them, but they'd gone and no one in there knew them or where they'd come from or where they were going. I drove around Taupo but there was no sign of them or their truck.

The next day I stuck an ad in the local paper and got them to run it three times. There was no response, and I soon got a good idea why. I'd done those blokes a favour. That dog was the most useless, thieving, sneaky, noisy, cowardly, mad-headed, untrainable, thick-skinned, exasperating mongrel of a thing I'd ever been stuck with.

If it was mine I wouldn't have hesitated to get one of my mates to put it and everyone else out of its misery, but it wasn't mine. I'd pinched it, and while there was a chance of its owner turning up I could hardly shoot the thing as well. So I had to put up with him.

I called him Guts, a name that had nothing to do with courage. I took him out with the rabbit-pack and he ran round barking his head off all morning. I managed to clobber him with a lump of wood and he ran back to the ute and jumped in the window and ate the Rabbit Board Inspector's lunch.

We decided to leave Guts in a cage on the ute for the rest of the day, but we couldn't catch him. We had to put all the dogs in the cages, all fifteen of them, and Guts got in amongst them. Then we let the others out and kept him in there. The boss asked me if I'd mind not bringing Guts out on the job again. He was too disruptive. I had to agree.

The next day I left Guts tied up and when I got home that night I found that he'd slipped his collar and killed four of my free-range chooks. The rooster and the other two chooks were clucking in fright in the branches of a big manuka tree. Guts was playfully tossing a dead chook around the yard.

In accordance with an ancient remedy I tied a dead chook around Guts' neck. It's supposed to cure them of chooks but it didn't even look like working with Guts. He seemed to like it. Used to roll in it. It got too disgusting in the finish so I cut it off and buried it. Guts dug it up again and rolled in it and then ate it, remaining feathers and all.

I spent half a day making a dog-proof netting cage to keep Guts in. He was too good at collar-slipping to be trusted. I now had him secured, when he was caged, but he had to be let out for a run and when he was out he was always getting up to mischief. He'd disappear for hours on end and I'd worry what he might be getting up to. With a bit of luck he might get pinched, or even shot.

Two mates of mine and I were going on a pig-hunt on the mountain and we met at my place. We had some reasonably good dogs but someone suggested bringing Guts to see what he was like on pigs. He had a few scars on him that looked like pig-rips. So we took him.

We got a couple of pigs that day, but no thanks to Guts. He was as useless on pigs as he was on everything else. He had scars on him because he was too gutless to go in on the pigs but too stupid to keep out of the way. He got bitten by a sow and ran away yelping. He ended up getting lost in the bush and howled his head off, scaring all the game for miles. We had to climb down into a dirty gully to get him. He was having trouble getting up a bank.

That dog was definitely one of the worst I ever knew, and he didn't improve. He tore a good mutton carcass I had hanging in a tree to bits. He dug up my lettuce seedlings. He bit my girlfriend. He chewed my hand-made cartridge-belt. He bullied my burrow-dog. He put a car off the road into the ditch. It just went on happening.

The final straw was when my neighbour's wife, nearly a mile down the road, came into her kitchen one day and found Guts head-down in her rubbish bin. She shouted at him and he must have got a fright because he ran yelping through the house and tried to jump through a window that was closed. The window cracked (I had to pay for it) and Guts upset quite a few other things before he made it back out the door.

This was it. I'd put up with three months of it. I'd paid dearly for my mistake. Besides, in all decency I couldn't pass a dog like Guts on to anyone else. He was a menace.

It was with a minimum of regret that I saw Guts disappear down the road on my mate's ute, on his way to where he'd do no further mischief. But even that was not to be. I found out later that my mate ran into someone who was trying to get a pack of dogs together and he gave Guts to him. My relief that Guts hadn't had to be shot after all was tempered by the thought that the useless bloody mongrel was still running around somewhere.

DAN

I'D LIKE TO tell you about one of the best dogs I've ever had. A mate and I were sent to hunt a winter block for pigs and when we got there we found a fairly serious situation. A deep snow boundary had come down on the Ruahine Ranges, trapping all these wild pigs in a wide bush and scrub valley between the mountains and the farms. There were literally hundreds of them and they were coming out onto the backs of the farms, doing a lot of damage to the fences and winter pastures.

The farmers were pleased to see us and offered us the free use of huts and horses, free mutton and dog tucker, anything we needed, just to get rid of those pigs. Two of the farmers tried to bribe us, with beef and the use of a tractor, to do their places first.

Johnny and I were both keen pig-hunters and eager to get on with the job. He had three big Airedale-cross dogs and I had two bull-mastiff-blue-heelers and two bitsers. Bits of this and bits of that. Mongrels.

We packed supplies in to one of the huts and got stuck into all this pig-hunting. At first we were going from pig to pig all day. Then the dogs started getting less keen on it. My big bulldogs' feet were always packing up and they were spending more time on the chain than hunting. Johnny's Airedales were getting badly cut around the ears and eyes from running through pig-tunnels in the fern all the time. After a while we only had enough fit dogs to make up one pack, so we hunted together.

76

One of my bitsers turned out to be the best pig-dog we had. He was a good finder, he could stop 'em and bail 'em or hold 'em. We caught a lot of pigs with him but he was a bit reckless with boars and was always getting knocked around. In fact the way he was going he had the life expectancy of a match.

Despite the cutback on our resources we were getting a lot of pigs. A hundred in a week was an average tail-count. Then we'd cleaned up all the easy pigs and found ourselves with a valley full of nasty boars that had nowhere to go. We knew they were there and they knew we were there, we'd had several brushes with most of them. We'd give all the dogs a day or two on the chain and starve them down a bit and then take both packs out after one of the boars. We got a few of them but with seven dogs on one pig in thick fern some of them had to get ripped up. At one stage we had five of them on the chain with various injuries. My good bitser got so badly ripped up one day that Johnny had to finish him off. Then one of my Bullies didn't come back from a chase after a boar that got away from us.

One day when we were out at a sheep station picking up some supplies one of the musterers asked me if I wanted a dog. I said sure, I'd give just about anything a go. It was a black and white border-collie heading dog called Dan. About six or seven years old, the musterer reckoned. It worked okay, a bit inclined to be hard on the stock. He just didn't have the work for him. Too many dogs.

I led Dan into the hut on a rope and tied him up and fed him. He was a surly kind of a dog and it was a week before he'd follow me anywhere. He got into a fight with one of my Bullies one day and to my surprise Dan beat him. Got him by a front leg and it was all over.

We took Dan out hunting a few times but he didn't seem very interested. Then a funny thing began to happen. Dan began to like me, accept me. He tolerated me patting him and feeding him. He watched me with his eyes wherever I moved. He followed first behind me on the track and wouldn't let any of the other dogs there.

Then one wet day when we were resting up the dogs I decided to walk over to another hut for a packful of supplies. Johnny was reading a book. I decided to take Dan with me because he was the only dog without sore feet and on the way he took off into the scrub and a bit later started barking in the gully.

I dropped my pack and sneaked down to see what he had there. Then I saw this dirty big boar standing in his nest at the edge of a clump of manuka, with Dan standing a few feet in front of him, barking steadily. He was an eye-dog and seemed to have the pig mesmerised. It never saw me, I dropped it where it was standing.

We knew that boar. It had carved up two of our dogs. If we'd put the pack onto it there would have been a hell of a stink, but it hadn't moved a foot from where Dan had found it.

Dan turned out to be the best hunting-dog I'd ever had. He understood what was wanted and tried his best to do it, and his best was pretty good. He was hunting for me and not for himself. I got as many pigs with just Dan on his own as Johnny did with all the other dogs. Dan always preferred to hunt on his own and wouldn't work in with the other dogs. He was aloof from them.

He was quick and hard. I saw him one day catch up to a boar in a clearing and grab it by the backside and spin it around and bail it hard till I got there. Anything he could handle he'd hold by the ear and anything too big to hold would get stopped and bailed. We hardly ever lost a pig.

I never had to raise my voice at Dan or tie him up around the hut. He never wandered away, he'd just sit somewhere where he could watch the door until I came out again.

By the end of the season you could hunt that valley all day

and come back empty-handed. We'd done a pretty good job. When the season ended I gave my other dogs to Johnny and kept Dan. Couldn't bear to part with him.

I moved down south and got a summer deer-hunting block. At the base hut I met my new mate and a Field Officer, who was looking after us for the season. "What's that dog doing here?" said the F.O.

"It's mine," I said.

"No dogs on the deer blocks," he said. "You'll have to get rid of it."

And before he left he said, "Make sure you get rid of that dog before I come back."

"Sure," I said.

Dan turned out to be a great deer-dog. The deer were resting up in the daytime in the leather-leaf gullies above the bush line. I'd climb up there and when Dan indicated that there were deer in a gully I'd prop myself up on a handy rock and say "Go on". Dan would trot down the ridge and get below the deer and then come quietly up on them. The deer had never seen a dog before and didn't know whether it was friend or foe. They'd come walking up out of the gully and stand looking back towards the dog. It was almost too easy. Some days I was getting thirty or forty deer, twice as many as my mate, who was getting up before daylight and hunting the river flats and then working the creeks all day and the flats again in the evenings.

After a month when the Field Officer returned with more supplies he was surprised at my tally.

"Where are you getting all these deer, Crumpy?"

"Along the tops, just above the bushline," I told him.

Just then he saw the dog.

"What's that bloody dog still doing here? I told you to get rid of it."

"I can't," I said. "I've been getting all my deer with him."

"I don't care," he said. "No dogs on the deer blocks. That's the rule. If it's still here when I come back I'll shoot the bloody thing myself."

"Sure," I said.

My shooting mate had had enough of it and was chucking in the job. The following day the F.O. and I loaded our packs and lugged them up onto the tops. We were going to stock up a bivvy three hours further along the range. We were resting our packs on a rocky ledge on top of the ridge. There were some deer in a scrubby gully just below us. Dan was indicating urgently – looking at me and down into the gully and then back at me.

"What's wrong with that bloody dog of yours?" asked the F.O.

"He's indicating," I said. "There's deer down in there. Load your rifle, we might as well get them."

He looked a bit sceptical but he loaded his gun and I told the dog, "go on", and off he trotted. A couple of minutes later two spikers came walking up out of the gully. They stopped right in front of us looking back into the gully. The F.O. dropped the both of them.

We got eighteen deer on the way to the bivvy that day and by the time we got there the F.O. was completely sold on dogs. I tried to explain to him that not all dogs were like Dan, but he can't have got the message because the next time he came he had a big scoffing yellow hooler of a dog he'd got off a pig-hunter.

"It's already been on deer," he said.

I said nothing. The next day Dan rousted four deer out of a gully. As soon as the F.O.'s new dog saw them it started barking madly and took off after them. Deer and dog vanished around the mountainside and we never saw or heard the F.O.'s deer-dog again. Over a bluff, would be my guess.

The F.O. tried two other dogs, one a red setter and the other a Labrador, before he gave up on it. I got just under four thousand deer that season, most of them with Dan, and I went on to hunt several more seasons with him. I caught literally thousands of pigs and deer with him and did quite a lot of stock-work. For six years he was my constant companion and best mate.

Finally, half-deaf, half-blind, half-fit but still fully loyal, Dan was retired to a friend's goat-stud farm, where, at last report, he wasn't taking any nonsense from those goats. In fact they reckon the goats have never been so easy to handle.

I still use working dogs for hunting and I've had some pretty good ones, but none of them could have held a candle to that old border-collie heading dog of mine, Dan.

WILD PORK

END OF THE deer season in the Urewera Country, 1955. The shooters from the various blocks assembled at the base camp. It was May and some of us had been in the bush since the previous October. We were looking forward to a spell in town. On the first day out of the bush most of the blokes got on the bus and went into Rotorua on their way to home or wherever they were going. I waited a couple of days for two mates who were a bit late coming off the Waikaremoana Block.

The only public transport that came through Ruatahuna was the New Zealand Railways Road Services bus, three times a week, and when we went to catch it into town we ran into a snag. There was a new bus driver and he didn't want us to put our pig-dogs in the luggage compartment. The old driver never minded but this new bloke was a bit fastidious about the rules. There were only half a dozen other people on the bus, all locals, they didn't mind, but the new driver took a fair bit of persuading. Finally, with rather ill grace, he let us stick our dogs in the back and off we went.

Out through the bushed ranges of the Urewera to Murupara and then off through the pine forests of Kaiangaroa on the road to Rotorua. All pumice and potholes.

About halfway through the forestry a big black pig ran across the road in front of the bus. We yelled at the driver to pull up, which he did rather reluctantly. Our old driver wouldn't have had to be told.

We ran round and let the dogs out and my two mates ran off into the pines after them while I paused to dig some ammunition out of my pack and grab a rifle. The driver was calling out something about not waiting and not having any pigs on the bus. I told him we'd only be a couple of minutes and took off after the others.

The pig was a boar and it got a fair way through the pines before the dogs pulled it up and bailed it in a patch of fern. I shot it and we gutted it and started dragging it out to the road. It was a good bit of pork. One of the dogs had been ripped in the neck and was losing a bit of blood, which wasn't going to please the bus driver much, but we needn't have worried about that because just before we got out to the fire-break at the edge of the road we heard the bus take off.

This was bloody lovely. Here we were, stranded with three dogs, a rifle and a dead pig in the middle of the Kaiangaroa pine forest, where you weren't supposed to hunt without a permit and not at all in the fire season. Our chances of getting a ride into town from here were pretty remote.

They were very toey about fire in the forestry and every high point had a manned fire-lookout, keeping the whole area under constant surveillance. There were severe penalties for any breaches of the fire regulations.

What did we do? Well, one of the blokes smoked and he had his tobacco and matches on him, so we built up a nice big fire in the middle of the fire-break and singed our pig on it, sending up a good big column of smoke in the process. We'd just finished the job when a ute came tearing along and pulled up and two blokes jumped out and doused our fire with an extinguisher before they even spoke to us.

The boss man was indignant. What the hell did we think we were doing, lighting a fire in the forestry? Where was our permit? What were we doing there anyway? What were our names?

We told him our names and he'd heard of me from his brother who I'd worked with in a timber mill the previous winter. He was a real good cobber of mine. That thawed the situation out a bit and we explained how we'd just stopped the bus to get the pig and the driver took off without us, and how our fire had been completely under control and hadn't been any danger to anything, and how all we needed now was a lift into town.

They gave us a lecture about how serious it was to light fires in the forestry and took us and our dogs and our pig to Rotorua, picked up our packs from the Road Services Depot and one of them who lived in Rotorua gave us a bunk for the night in his spare room. That night at his place we met some people who were preparing a hangi for the next day and we gave them our pig.

We wouldn't let them pay us for the pig so they invited us to the hangi, where one of my mates met and fell in love with a pretty Maori girl. He ended up getting married, gave up hunting and moved onto the in-laws' dairy farm over near Wanganui. I heard they raised a large family.

At the same hangi my other mate hit it off with a bloke who needed an off-sider on his fishing boat. They left for Tauranga the next day and I never saw my mate again. A few years later I heard he was still on the fishing boats.

And it was at that same hangi that I met my good friend old Norm Rata, who took me under his wing and taught me all I know about felling trees with a crosscut saw and splitting posts and battens and strainers with axe and maul. It was two years before I got back into serious hunting.

So there it was. A pig runs across a road in front of a bus and puts three professional hunters out of business. Altered the course of our lives forever. A wild bit of pork, that!

STRAWBERRY JAM

I sit alone at breakfast in a hotel dining room, looking through a little wicker basket on the table for something to put on a piece of toast. There are sachets of butter, honey, Vegemite, marmalade – and strawberry jam. Strawberry jam. It always triggers the same memories in me . . .

WHEN I WAS at high school I had a paper round, paying off a pushbike at ten bob a week. There were four of us boys delivering morning papers around the small town we lived in. They provided us with green canvas bags that hung across the bar of the bike to carry the papers in. We'd count out our papers and put them in the bag and ride around the streets, rolling up papers tightly and bending the roll so it wouldn't come undone, and firing them into the front porches of the houses. We got pretty good at it, especially when it was raining because if you missed you had to stop and do it properly.

In the winter it was still dark when we arrived at the corner where the early bus dropped off the bundles of papers. One of the boys' father had the bakery just along the street and while we were waiting for the bus we'd nip along there and get stuck into the bread rolls that hadn't turned out right. It was a real good place on a cold morning, warm and full of the smell of freshly-baked bread, pastry, savouries and stuff. We'd butter the rolls and put jam on them from a four-gallon tin behind the door. Strawberry jam. It was about two-thirds full with a round lid in the top of it and we'd scoop the knife through it and smear it on the rolls and eat as many of them as we could before the

85

bus came along. Fresh hot bread rolls with butter and jam dripping from them. It was delicious.

We'd been doing this for weeks, until one morning when one of the boys reached into the jam tin and scooped the knife through it and lifted it out into the light with the disintegrating carcase of a big bakery rat draped across it, bones sticking out and patches of bare white skin where the hair had fallen out. We all stopped chewing in mid-chew and looked at each other, realising what those funny bits were that we'd been noticing in the jam lately.

We stood like that for a few soul-blistering moments. The boy with the rat on the knife shouted "NO!" and dropped it on the floor, and suddenly we were all running out into the street, spitting and gagging and coughing and retching. One of the boys was sick in the gutter. I gagged and spat all the way round my round that morning, trying to get the taste of that jam out of my mouth. After that strawberry jam was definitely off the menu as far as I was concerned. It wasn't hard to keep away from, but I couldn't think about the stuff without remembering that rat.

My memory then skips eight years on to when I was culling deer for the government in the back country. We'd been packing all our gear and supplies into our blocks on our backs, an arduous process, and now, for the first time, we were to have air-drops. A gutsy pilot called Popeye Lucas would fly into the valleys in a little Auster aeroplane with one door off. A bloke would sit with his back to the pilot and when Popeye shouted "Now!" he'd throw out the sacks of supplies attached to small supply-chutes. They'd circle at about two thousand feet until all the bags were thrown out. Twenty-five-pound bags of flour were put inside several sacks and free-dropped.

I'd been given a deer-block in a heavily-bushed valley five hours' walk in from the road and I was to receive my first air-drop of supplies in there. I backpacked in tentage for a camp, an axe, some rope, sleeping bag, clothes, ammunition and a small amount of food to keep me going until the plane arrived.

At a prearranged place called the Te Waiotukapiti Forks I dumped my two-hundred-pound pack and prepared a fire out on the riverbed, ready to light when the plane came so the pilot could see where the smoke drifted. Then I set about building the tent camp with poles cut from the bush for a frame, lashed together with rope.

It rained on and off for the first few days but I'd been told not to go away from the camp in case the cloud lifted and the plane could get in. I filled in the time splitting tawa and building a wooden chimney at one end of the tent and lining it with flat rocks from the riverbed. I built two bunks and a table and cut a big pile of firewood and stacked it up to dry. Still the plane didn't come.

In five days I was out of food. There were deer and pigs within half an hour's walk of the camp but I dared not go away hunting, just in case. I shot a trout in the river and two pigeons in the trees (not illegal when it's a matter of survival). It's not safe to let your energy get too low when you're on your own in the bush.

Still the plane couldn't get in. There was a ceiling of cloud across the valley and no wind to blow it away. I was saving my last stub of candle to get the fire out on the riverbed going, so after dark I had only firelight. So much for these new-fangled air-drops. I had isolation, hunger, enforced idleness and now darkness to endure. I might as well have had a broken leg. By this time I could have walked back out to the road and packed in a load of supplies and got on with my hunting.

I'd been there for eleven days before the cloud lifted. About mid-morning I heard the plane coming. I ran out and lit the fire and the plane circled above me. Parachutes began to drift down and I drew lines in a patch of sand to indicate where each chute landed in the bush. Then the plane flew across low and free-dropped two bags of flour. One of them hit my camp right near the ridge-pole and went through the tent and exploded out through the chimney, demolishing it, but when you've had nothing to eat for three days you don't worry about little things like that. It could be fixed.

I ripped open the handiest bag of food. It had nothing in it but tins of strawberry jam. I gathered up more bags and opened one of them. More strawberry jam. I collected all the bags, including two I had to climb trees to retrieve, and opened them. They'd dropped me ninety-eight tins of strawberry jam and two bags of flour, a camp oven and three billies. It had to be some kind of weird joke!

I found out later that there'd been a mix-up out at the woolshed where they were making up the air-drops. The bloke in the next valley to me got all the condensed milk. Two blokes on another block got all the tinned peas. By a cruel twist of fate I'd got the strawberry jam.

What do you do when you're starving and all you've got to eat is damper and strawberry jam? You eat it, that's what you do. When I'd had a few feeds to get a bit of energy back I went out and shot some deer and feasted on flour and water, meat and jam, rebuilt the chimney, laced sacks over the hole in the tent and then set about building up a deer tally. By this time I'd completely overcome my repugnance for strawberry jam. I'd have eaten it even if there'd been a rat in it. Great stuff when there's nothing else to eat!

After a week they flew in and dropped me supplies of tea, milk, sugar, spuds, onions, yeast, rice, cheese, peas and dried fruit. The strawberry jam diet was over.

Grinning to myself at the memory I open the sachet of strawberry jam and spread it on my toast and sink my teeth into it. Across the dining room I see a couple staring at me, wondering what on earth I could be finding so humorous about breakfast in a hotel. I grin some more at the idea of what they'd think if I went over there and told them it was the strawberry jam. But no, the bit about the rat might put them off their tucker.

Enjoy your lunch, won't you.

THE DROVER

I WAS DROVING a mob of cattle from a station down the coast to the saleyards in Gisborne, under the wing of an old stockman called Bob who'd been working with sheep and cattle all his life. He was one of the old breed and had some fairly old-fashioned ideas. He didn't like suggestions, but I soon found out not to offer any and we got along okay. He was a taciturn sort of bloke but he had a short fuse and lost his rag a lot, with the result that he was either shouting at me or his dogs or saying nothing at all. He was okay though.

This night the mob was in the holding paddock, the dogs were tied up and fed and the horses were chomping the grass outside the hut we were using. This was our last night on the road, our cattle were being trucked the rest of the way.

He wasn't much of a talker, old Bob. I'd been working with him for three weeks and still knew nothing about him except that he'd worked on sheep and cattle stations all his life and still couldn't cook a mutton chop properly, and he cursed men and dogs in his sleep. We were sitting in front of the fire with after-dinner mugs of tea in our hands.

"We nearly lost a couple of them over that cliff today," I remarked.

Bob grunted, and then after a few moments he said, "Lost the whole mob once."

"Eh?" I was intrigued.

His story was a bit rusty at first but it gathered momentum as he got into telling it. He'd been brought up in a West Coast farming community of four families and this happened when he was seventeen.

They'd had a hell of a storm and the only cattle track in and out of the bay they lived in was washed out and blocked by windfalls. Bob and another young bloke, a cousin of his, were sent to drive the cattle from all four farms up the coast to the annual cattle sale. They'd taken stock up and down the coast before and never had any trouble with them and they weren't expecting any this time. They had eight cattle dogs and rode experienced stock-horses.

The first day went off all right. They camped the cattle on the beach that night and when the tide was out the next morning they pushed them round the headland into the next bay and made good progress up the coast. That evening they made their big mistake. The sun was sinking on the horizon and the tide was coming in but they decided to shove the mob round into the next bay for the night, to save having to wait for the tide in the morning.

The cattle were getting used to the sea and they'd already swum across two rivers. They were belly deep as they rounded an outcrop of rock and when the swells lifted them they started swimming. The leaders swam straight out towards the setting sun and the rest of the mob followed them. There was nothing Bob and his cousin could do to stop them or turn them around. Their dogs couldn't even get out through the surf. They could only stand on the beach and watch four hundred and sixteen prime steers, the whole year's beef production from four farms, swim out into the Tasman Sea and disappear into the gathering twilight. Thirty thousand quid's worth of them.

This was going to be a serious financial blow to the whole community. It could easily be the ruin of them, no farm could survive that kind of loss. Bob and his cousin camped on the beach and discussed whether to emigrate or not. In those days there was only one place the blame was going – right on them. They were in deep trouble.

The next day they had to wait for the tide to go out before they could set off back down the coast to break the bad news to their folks. As they splashed round the headland and came in sight of the next bay they got the surprise of their lives. Their cattle were feeding along the bush edge at the top of the beach. They put the dogs round them and herded them up. They were all there. There was relief in Bob's voice as he told me about it all those years later.

He reckoned that what must have happened was that the cattle swam towards the brightest light they could see in the dusk, and when the sun went below the horizon the brightest light they could then see was the last of the sunlight on the mountain range behind the beach, so they turned and swam towards that. The tide carried them down the coast and they came ashore in the next bay.

They got them to the saleyards without any further mishaps, but they didn't tell anybody about how they'd lost the whole lot of them until a long time after it had happened.

I did two more droving jobs with old Bob and we got to know each other quite well. He thawed out once he got to know you and had many interesting stories to tell about the pioneering days of farming in the back country, but his best yarn was always that first one about the disappearing mob of cattle.

LAST LAUGH

THERE'S AN OLD saying that goes, *He who laughs last, laughs longest,* but in this yarn it's a case of *He whose laugh lasts, laughs longest,* and it concerns my first serious girlfriend and I. We were living in a poky little flat in Ponsonby. I was driving trucks and she was waitressing. She was a good sort and had a great sense of humour and we had a lot of fun together.

We saved money and bought a car, for forty-five quid, a '38 Chevrolet sedan, the first model with the headlights set down in the front mudguards, in-line six-cylinder motor and hydraulic brakes. A good car. It was nearly twenty years old when we got it but there were still quite a few of them around and the parts were easy to get.

This day we both had the day off work. I had to go and see a lawyer about an accident I'd witnessed and my girlfriend said she wanted to get a couple of things so we drove into town and parked. We were going to meet back at the car and then go and have a bit of lunch somewhere.

When I got back to the car there was no sign of my girlfriend so I got in to sit and wait for her, and the first thing I noticed were some packages wrapped in fancy paper on the back seat. What the hell was she up to? She knew we couldn't afford to go buying stuff.

I tore the paper off a package and found a pair of pink fluffy bedroom slippers in it. Another parcel had a frilly blouse thing in it. Another had table mats and serviettes. Nothing we needed. What the hell was the woman up to? She must have flipped her lid! I ripped open another package and revealed a label that informed me I was holding a dozen nappies made of one hundred per cent pure cotton.

That rocked me. No one had said anything to me about needing any nappies. I threw the torn paper and opened parcels onto the back seat and sat there thoughtfully drumming my fingers on the steering wheel. My future stretched out in front of me and I didn't like the look of it. I didn't mind kids but the thought of having one of my own had never occurred to me. What was I going to do with it? I wasn't ready for fatherhood.

Then I noticed the car key. In those days you never locked your car or took the keys out of it, but this key had a little fluffy doll thing hanging from it. I'd never seen it before. Come to think of it I'd never seen this car before, either. I was in the wrong bloody car, and I'd ripped open all their shopping.

Greatly relieved I got out of the car and closed the door. There was our car five cars along the street with my girlfriend sitting in it waiting for me. Not pregnant. Just then a woman came running up demanding to know what I was doing in their car. She'd seen me getting out of it. Then she saw the mess her parcels were in and started calling me a thief.

I was trying to explain when her husband turned up, a big bloke, and she told him how she'd seen me getting out of their car and look what I'd done to her things. The big husband got right to the heart of the matter.

"What the hell do you think you're comin' at?" he said.

"No big deal mate," I told him. "I just got in the wrong car, that's all. That's my car just along there."

The woman was going on about what I'd done to her lovely things. They were presents for her sister, who was having a baby.

"Yeah," said the big husband. "What do you want to go rippin' open that stuff for?"

I was groping for an answer to that when two policemen on their beat came along and wanted to know what was going on. The woman immediately dobbed me in, told the policemen all about it and showed them the mess I'd made of her parcels. To make explanation tougher my girlfriend saw me and came along to see what was happening, doing her best to keep a straight face.

"Did you do this?" one of the policemen said to me, pointing at the mess in the car.

I'd never felt so stupid.

"Yes," I said. "But I didn't know it was theirs."

"Whose did you think it was?"

"I thought my girlfriend here had bought it."

"Well you're going to have to get it wrapped up again aren't you?" asked the policeman.

In the finish I gave the woman a quid to get five bob's worth of paper wrapped around her stuff and we all went on our way. I would have soon forgotten all about the incident, but my girlfriend wouldn't let me. Women have incredible memories for things like that and she gave me heaps about it. She thought it was a hoot and cracked up whenever she thought of it, conveniently forgetting about things like the time somebody gave her a chicken, a live one, and she decided to prepare it for cooking, so she donged it on the head with a rolling pin and began to pluck it. Suddenly the chook came to life and took off, flapping and squawking around the flat with half its feathers missing. She didn't think that was at all funny, but she never got tired of telling people about my little mistake over the car, staggering around doubled over with mirth and slapping at her legs.

The girlfriend and I eventually split up, but we're good mates and we've kept in touch over the years. She married a bloke who became a good friend of mine. They've got a kiwifruit

95

orchard in the Bay of Plenty and I've worked for them a few times. I usually call in to see them when I'm through that way. They reared two kids, a boy and a girl, both married now with kids of their own.

The last time I called in on them their son and his wife were visiting and there were three grandkids running around. One of them, a six-year-old shaver, and I were giving my dog a run on the beach and as we walked along he said,

"Uncle Crumpy?"

"What mate?"

"Did you really get in somebody's wrong car and open all their Christmas presents?"

I had to think for a few moments to remember.

"Something like that," I said. "Who told you about it?"

"Granny. She thinks it's funny."

"So do I," I said, grinning at the thought of someone still laughing at something that happened a third of a century before.

He whose laugh lasts definitely laughs the longest. I'm glad I never told her about the napkins and the fright they'd given me.

Sixpence an Hour

I N 1959 I started writing my first book, *A Good Keen Man*. My girlfriend, Jean, and I were living in a poky little bed-sitter in a back street at the time. Jean was working in a printery and I'd thrown in my driving job and sat at home working on what I jokingly referred to as 'The Great New Zealand Novel'. I wrote it in longhand in exercise books and then spent a month picking it out with my two forefingers on an ancient borrowed Imperial 66 typewriter, altering it as I went. I still write that way, except that the typewriter is more up-to-date these days.

At last it was finished. Now all I had to do was get it published. From what I could find out there were three publishers of books in New Zealand at that time, Pauls and Whitcombe and Tombes in Auckland, and A.H. and A.W. Reed in Wellington. One of them might take it on. The morning after it was completed I went to the printery where Jean worked and got them to staple the one copy of my priceless manuscript together. Then I took it down Queen Street to the premises of Pauls Books and found the head bloke's office.

I explained to the receptionist that I'd written this here book and would they be interested in publishing it. She took it into the office, where the head bloke was sitting just out of sight from me through the open door, and told him what I'd told her. There was a bit of mumbling and she came back and gave the book to me and said they weren't interested in publishing any books at the moment. He hadn't even looked at it.

I took it up the street to Whitcombe and Tombes, where I got to see a Mr Whitcombe Himself. He said he'd read my manuscript and let me know. He wrote my address down and said he'd be in touch by mail in a week or two. At least he'd agreed to read the thing. If you've ever left your newborn baby with a shady-looking stranger you'll know what it's like to leave the only copy of your first novel with a bloke who tells you he'll 'be in touch'.

We hadn't had much money coming in while I'd been writing and I had to get a job to bring the rent and food situation back to square. Every day I'd rush home from work to see what was in the mail. It was three weeks before my manuscript arrived in a package, with a letter from Mr Whitcombe saying,

Dear Mr Crump
Thank you for submitting your manuscript, which we have
read with interest. We regret, however, that the
publication of this book would be profitable neither to
you nor ourselves.
I herewith return your mss. Thanking you.
Yours faithfully
Alex Whitcombe

So that was that.

There was only one other publisher left to try. I sent my book to A.H. and A.W. Reed in Wellington. If they turned it down I was going to forget about getting it published. I'd got a lot of satisfaction from the writing of it and it had been worth it for that.

Several weeks went by and we got on with our lives, and then a letter arrived from a Mr Richards at Reeds. They'd like to publish my book, the letter said, providing I was prepared to go through it with a journalist they would employ to help me 'knock it into shape'. I was insulted at the suggestion that my writing wasn't good enough and immediately replied to Mr Richards that I would be only too happy to comply with his requirements.

Jean and I decided to move down to Wellington and follow up this adventure. She was more excited at the prospect of us getting a book published than I was. The car we had at the time was a clapped-out 1934 V8 and I was always working on it to keep it on the road. We didn't have enough money to get there, but we loaded our few possessions into the car and set off for Wellington.

We slept in the car for two nights in Hamilton while I found and fitted a second-hand head gasket, and we got towed into Rotorua with a con-rod through the side of the block. Jean got a job on the staff of Brent's Hotel and I worked for the Council putting fences around thermal mud pools and geysers. At night I ringbolted in Jean's room in the hotel staff quarters.

We had the V8 parked in the yard behind the hotel and it was a month before I'd found, paid for and fitted another motor in it. That left us broke again so we worked there for another month to get a bit of a stake together.

We'd kept Mr Richards acquainted with our progress towards Wellington and we set off again having told him by phone we'd see him in a couple of days, but it turned out to be more like a couple of weeks. The new/second-hand motor went good, too good for the transmission and we were towed into Palmerston North with a grunted gearbox.

The wreckers had to get a gearbox sent up from Levin and it was three days and thirty quid before we were able to continue on our journey, and then we had to stop in Bulls because the differential was chewed out. It took three more days to find and fit another diff and after that we had just enough money left for gas to get us into Wellington. We'd made it.

By the time we parked our rebuilt Ford outside Reeds Publishing House in Taranaki Street we'd spent more on it than it was worth. It had taken us two months and two weeks to drive from Auckland to Wellington. Later on I did the same trip on a Kawasaki motorbike in six hours.

We presented ourselves at Mr Richards' office, greasy, unkempt and unwashed from sleeping in the car. He must have wondered what the cat had dragged in but he didn't turn a hair. His secretary got us cups of coffee and Mr Richards explained how he'd arranged for a good journalist to help me knock my book into shape and we should give him a ring when we'd settled in. He was a bit shocked to learn that he had the only copy of the book that existed.

I'd had the notion of possibly tapping him for some kind of advance, but I could tell from his talk that any kind of payment was still a long way off, possibly a year. He told us about the huge risks they were taking, printing, illustrators, journalists, advertising and distribution – thousands and thousands of pounds. It made us feel humble. A man could hardly tap him for five quid on account in the face of all that.

We slept in the car for the first week. Jean got a job waitressing and I got one driving earthmoving machinery on the Wellington airport project. We mostly ate leftovers from the restaurant Jean worked in and I snipped my boss for a tank of gas so I could get back and forth to work. With Jean's first pay we rented a room in a boarding house and with mine we started eating properly again. I was getting sick of stale cakes and cold pies.

The journalist Mr Richards had engaged to help me knock my novel into shape was a bloke called Alex, who also lived in a little back-street room. His advice made sense to me and he was greatly relieved when he realised I was prepared to have my stuff altered around. We became good friends and for several months spent most of our evenings shuffling the material into sequence and eliminating repetition and filling in gaps and generally getting the book to flow. I learnt a lot from Alex and later when I showed him my second book before giving it to Reeds he said he wouldn't alter it in any way, so what he'd taught me must have sunk in.

Finally *A Good Keen Man* was ready for publication, a year after it had first been tentatively accepted. It was illustrated by Dennis Knight-Turner, who illustrated my next four books as well. Mr Richards shook hands with us in his office and told us the book was in the process of being printed by Halstead Press in Australia and would be in the bookshops within a month. He handed me a cheque for £100 advance royalties and asked us if we thought we had fifty friends who might buy the book. We didn't know.

A hundred quid! That was big money to us, and I really felt as though I'd earned it. It worked out at about sixpence an hour for the time I'd put in on it. We used the £100 cheque for a deposit on a 1945 V8 ute with hydraulic brakes. It even had a radio in it! We got fifteen quid off a wrecker for our old car, less than a quarter of what it had cost us to get the thing from Auckland to Wellington. Within days Jean and I were packed up and headed for a rabbiting job we'd been accepted for in Pongaroa in the Wairarapa.

That was all there was to that particular adventure as far as I was concerned at the time. I'd written a book and had it published and been paid for it. There might even be more money in it yet, but the main and lasting thing was the satisfaction of having done it.

Today, thirty-five years later, *A Good Keen Man* is still in print and has sold more than two hundred and seventy-five thousand copies, but no subsequent royalty payment has ever given me the pleasure of that first cheque for a hundred quid. Sixpence an hour and no complaints.

THE FABULOUS FRITTER

FRESH SEAFOOD ALWAYS goes down well with me. I can handle heaps of it and I've put away a fair bit of it in my time, but there was one feed of kaimoana I'll never forget. I remember it as the adventure of the fabulous fritter.

My first full whitebaiting season was in the late sixties. My wife and I had the two front stands on the Black River in a very beautiful part of South Westland, and although it was an idyllic setting it was a hell of a place to get to. The only access to the river mouth was two deep wheel tracks full of water and mud that wound for nine miles through kahikatea bush and swamp.

There were five stands on the Black that season and all the supplies were brought in and the whitebait taken out by a young Coaster on a clapped-out Nuffield tractor with a narrow platform built around it to carry stuff on. There was no way you'd ever tow a trailer on that track, the ruts were too deep, and getting deeper every time the tractor went through them.

Everything had to be tied down on the tray round the tractor because many of the holes were so deep he had to charge through them to avoid getting bellied in the middle, bouncing and jolting in a great shower of mud and water. In one place the track crossed a small creek that kept bogging up and if you could charge through that without having to cut a platform of pungas you plunged into a wall of flax bushes and for a half a mile you couldn't see the track at all, because the flax hung right over it. I asked the driver how he could tell where the track was and he said he knew where it was before the flax grew over it.

Despite the heavy going, a lot of it through mud too deep for gumboots, it was easier and safer to walk than to ride on the tractor. The track ended a mile short of our stands and everything had to be carried from there along a walking track cut through the bush. We got our camp and whitebait stands set up and settled into whitebaiting, and my wife and I didn't see the road for three months. We just didn't need anything bad enough to make it worth walking that track for.

There was plenty of wildlife at the mouth of the Black. A big row of golden kowhai trees grew along the riverbank in front of our camp, filled with dozens of native pigeons and tuis putting on a constant display against the snowy Alps in the distance. There were deer and seals and wekas and penguins, trout and snapper and kahawai and flounder, mussels, kina, cockles and paua, a morepork in the moonlight and a possum on the roof.

There were also whitebait in moderate quantities coming into the river on some tides. We had one brief 'run' of them, which was exciting. A black band of whitebait streaming up the river and into your nets until they were sizzling full.

All in all it was a pleasant and successful season, although we were so pleased to see the road again at the end of it that we put ourselves on motorbikes and toured the country from one end to the other. I'd eaten something like two hundred whitebait fritters in those three months, and I still wasn't sick of them, and I still hadn't crossed paths with the fabulous fritter.

Twenty years and many fritters later I was cruising down the Coast following the travels of two fictitious characters I was writing about. I'd been camping out and some of my gear was wet so I decided to book into the Haast Hotel and have a clean up and a dry out and a feed that hadn't come out of a can.

I checked in and when I drove along to the room there was

a Jet-Ranger helicopter parked on the lawn outside the units. It belonged to two blokes who were staying in the unit next to mine. The publican introduced me to them in the bar that night and we got yarning.

They were whitebaiters. They had a stand at the mouth of a creek down the coast that you could only get to by chopper. They had the whole place to themselves. They'd flown across from Christchurch that morning and spent the day setting up their stand and getting their nets and screens ready. Tomorrow they were going to get stuck into it, and insisted that I come with them. By the end of the evening I'd agreed to.

Early the next morning I woke the whitebaiters and while the chopper was warming up we loaded it with boxes of food, gear, and beer. As the sun touched on the highest peaks of the Alps, we lifted off and followed the beach down the coast. We choppered past the end of the road at Jackson Bay and a bit further down the coast we swung into a small bay and put her down on a sandbar at the mouth of a small bushed stream.

It was a good-looking set-up all right. In great expectation we unloaded the chopper and retrieved the nets from the bush and set them in the edge of the stream. The fire was lit and the pan got ready for the production of special-recipe fresh whitebait fritters.

I'd decided to keep my mouth shut about whitebaiting because it'd been a long time since I'd done it and things were probably quite different now. These blokes seemed to know what they were doing. Using a helicopter like this had me impressed, especially when I remembered what we'd had to go through to get to our stands on the Black River. It was a bit slow at first, but that was nothing to worry about, I was told. The bait always comes in on the turn of the tide round here. So we had a cup of tea and some hotel corned-beef sandwiches and waited for the tide.

The tide came and went and by one o'clock in the afternoon we still hadn't caught any whitebait, so we ate the rest of the hotel lunch and washed it down with cans of beer. We were sitting on a washed-up log talking about big whitebait runs we'd seen or heard about and every now and again someone would wander across and check the nets. Nothing. Not one whitebait.

The tide turned again. Still nothing. If they didn't run by this time round here, I was told, they weren't going to run at all that day. We might as well wrap it up and give it another go tomorrow, they had to be running by then. So we stashed the nets in the bush and loaded up the chopper and blatted back up the coast to the hotel. We hadn't seen a whitebait.

The next day we went through the same procedure, and got nearly as few whitebait as the day before. The day wore on. We'd run out of whitebait yarns and predictions about time and tide and we were thinking of chucking it in for the day when a tiny shoal of whitebait swam up the creek and into one of the nets. Half a cupful at the most. This caused great excitement in the ranks.

"They're starting to run!" shouted one of the whitebaiters, up to his knees in the water peering into the net. "Get the pan ready!"

The pan was got ready but no more whitebait came. We gave it another half hour, but nothing. We poured the pathetic handful of bait into a bowl. It was prepared and cooked and we ate a third of it each, carefully shared out, almost to the last whitebait. It wasn't a bad little fritter, but when you look at what went into getting it, that has to be the most expensive three mouthfuls of food I've ever eaten.

Great stuff, we all agreed. This is the life! Wouldn't be dead for quids! We lifted the nets and loaded the chopper and flew back up the coast to the hotel.

"At least we're not going back empty-handed," one of the whitebaiters said to me.

"Er – no," I agreed.

I didn't go with our intrepid whitebaiters the next day, my fictional characters were getting badly side-tracked. The truth was turning out to be stranger than any fiction I could have dreamed up, so I continued on my travels. A few days later I heard that the whitebait had started running on the coast, so hopefully my two whitebaiting buddies were able to improve the cost-effectiveness of their operation.

They'd need to. When you add up the cost of seven hours of helicopter time, nine nights of hotel accommodation, meals, drinks and man-hours, that whitebait fritter had cost something like eight thousand dollars, about a thousand dollars a mouthful, more than a hundred dollars for each whitebait. At that rate, to get a pound of whitebait would have cost those blokes more than sixty thousand dollars. A fabulously expensive fritter, that one.

A DEAD CERT

"You coming to the races tomorrow, Crumpy?" my old mate Charlie Poweka asked me the other day.

"No," I said. "I don't bother with them."

"Had a bad run of luck eh?"

"No," I told him. "I'm just not temperamentally suited to gambling on racehorses, that's all."

"Why, when did you last go to a race meeting?"

"Nineteen fifty-nine," I told him. "That was the first and only time I ever had a bet on a racehorse, and that was by accident."

M**Y MEMORY FLICKED** back to a dark Friday night more than thirty years before. A mate of mine and I had been spotlighting for deer in the Kaiangaroa Forest. We'd got four and I dropped my mate and the venison off in Murupara and headed back towards Rotorua, where I was living. The main road was still waiting to be tarsealed – all pumice, potholes and corrugations.

It was about two-thirty in the morning and trying to start raining. Suddenly I had to swerve to avoid running into the back of an unlit horse-float parked in the roadway. As I swung round it my headlights lit up an old bloke in gumboots and a big hat, standing beside an old Chev car the horse-float was hitched to.

I stopped to see if he was all right. He wasn't. Those old cars had a six-volt system with the battery suspended in a metal cage under the car. His cage had rusted through and the battery had dropped out onto the road and he'd run over it. He was well and truly stuck there.

He was a sheep farmer and he'd come over from the Hawke's Bay, taking a horse to a race meeting that was on in Rotorua later that day. You could hear the horse stamping around in the float and kicking at the door.

We decided that I'd have to tow him to Rotorua. The only snag at this stage was that neither of us had a tow rope. I knew where there was an old fence a couple of miles up a side road near there. I'd climbed over it with a deer we'd shot earlier that night. We drove along there and twisted a length of number-eight wire out of the fence and took it back to his car and tied it to the tow-bar of my old Land Rover with four strands of it.

It was a long, heavy, jerky tow, with the horse-float and all, and it wasn't helped by the old bloke standing on his brakes every time we came to a bend in the road. He was a lousy driver. Long before we got to Rotorua I could smell my clutch burning out. By the time we got there I could hardly keep us moving and I was driving along with my head out the window to try and avoid the choking stink of burning clutch-plates.

I pulled him into the racetrack and stopped. It was just beginning to get daylight. We had to break off the wire, which had tightened around my towball.

"What's that smell?" said the old bloke.

"My clutch," I told him. "It's burnt out."

"Look mate," he said, lowering his voice confidentially and looking around as though someone might overhear him. "You've been bloody decent about this. If you want to make a few quid just stick some money on this horse of mine in the steeplechase today. It's going to win and it'll pay a good price. Its name's Pangola. It's a dead cert. You can't go wrong."

"Sure mate," I said.

I'd heard of these dead certs before and I wasn't going

to have any spare money to put on one of them.

Even free of the load I had trouble getting the Land Rover to move. I nursed it home and got in a couple of hours' sleep, and when the town came to life I crept along to a garage where I knew the blokes and got them to have a look at it. The clutch was absolutely grunted. A new clutch assembly was going to cost me three hundred and fifty quid by the time it was installed.

I left the Land Rover there and wandered off and had some breakfast and ended up in the public bar of the Grand Hotel with a beer in front of me, wondering where I was going to get three hundred and fifty quid. I had less than a hundred. It looked as though I might have to sell the Land Rover.

Later that day I was just leaving the pub when in walked Scrubby Rhodes, an old fencing and scrub-cutting mate of mine. I hardly recognised him at first. He was done up like a dog's dinner.

"What are you all dressed up for, Scrubby?" I asked him over a beer. "Somebody die?"

"No," he said. "I'm going to the races. Why don't you come?"

I wasn't keen but I had nothing else to do, so off we went on Scrubby's old Norton motor bike. The meeting was well underway by the time we got there. The fourth race was due to start and the horses were parading around behind the starting barrier. Scrubby went off to try to get a bet on. I made my way over to lean on the rails and watch the race, and found myself just along from the old bloke I'd towed in the night before, still in his gumboots and big hat. He spotted me.

"G'day mate," he said conspiratorially. "Did you get your money on this horse of mine? That's him there. Number nine, Pangola."

I looked at the horse and wondered how they'd ever let him enter it in a race. It was a big raw-boned gelding, covered with dried mud, jug-headed and dozy-looking. It was wandering around not taking much interest in anything. It was slightly apart from all the other horses and looked to me as though it needed drenching. The jockey was a young bloke who looked distinctly embarrassed, and I didn't blame him.

"What happened to its tail?" I asked the old bloke.

"The calves have been chewing it," he said. "But don't worry about that horse. It's a dead cert. It's got terrific stamina. It's paying more than twenty to one. How much did you put on it?"

"Well, nothing, actually," I stammered. "I only just got here."

"Hell," he said. "It's too late now, the tote's closed. That's no good. Here, take a few of these."

He took a big wad of tickets out of his pocket and thumbed off some of them and gave them to me.

"There, that ought to cover what it cost you."

Glancing across at the horse I accepted the tickets. If he wanted to waste his money like that I wasn't going to stop him. It had started raining. I turned up the collar of my coat. The old bloke chuckled gleefully.

"He goes good in a bit of heavy going," he confided. "The more mud the better he likes it."

Scrubby came and found me. He'd missed the tote.

"I'm going to put ten bob on a horse in the next race," he said. "Let's get in out of this rain."

"I think I'll hang on here," I said. "I've got tickets on one of these horses."

"Which one?"

"Number nine there. Pangola."

Scrubby stared incredulously at it and then consulted his race book.

"That thing!" he blurted. "It's a goat of a thing, a rank

outsider! You've blown your money. What made you go and back a thing like that?"

"I got a tip on it," I said weakly.

They started the race. It was a three-mile steeplechase. It was immediately obvious that Pangola couldn't jump. He clambered across the fences and regained his feet on the other side, with the poor jockey clinging desperately to his back. Surely he couldn't keep this up.

The first time the field thundered past us there was one bunch of horses, then fifty yards back to Pangola on his own, and then the rest of them fifty yards behind him. It was as though they didn't want to associate with him. He was pounding along in a shambling gallop, flinging mud and grass high into the air with every stride.

The second time they came past Pangola was up behind the leading bunch, still at the same pace. Some of the horses had fallen at the fences but not the one that should have. He was still miraculously on his feet. And the third time they came past Pangola was fifty yards ahead of the rest of them and pulling away, still at the same clumsy pace. If he stayed on his feet for the last three fences he was going to win it.

And he did. There wasn't another horse in the straight when Pangola blundered past the post. He was up at the next bend before the jockey could get him pulled up and turned around. He rode him back to the birdcage. The horse still had plenty of go in him. The white-faced jockey was having trouble holding him in.

"There y'are," grinned the old bloke. "I told you he was a dead cert! I'd better go and get him. He's a bit hard to handle when he's worked up."

"Hell Crumpy!" said Scrubby. "Who put you onto that horse?"

"That old bloke who was just here," I said. "He's the owner."

"How much did you have on it?"

"I don't know," I said. "He just gave me these tickets in return for towing him here last night. He'd broken down in the forestry."

I took the tickets out of my pocket. They were all five pounds for a win on number nine, ten of them. Pangola had paid twenty-two pounds ten. I didn't believe it until I'd collected the money at the tote, which was easy enough to do. There was no one else at the pay-out windows. I came away with eleven hundred and twenty-five pounds in my pocket.

I tried to get to the old bloke to thank him and offer him some of the money back but he was in the birdcage trying to control his horse among a crowd of people and I couldn't get near him.

Scrubby borrowed five quid off me and went off to place a bet on the next race. I'd had enough. I left the race track and got a taxi back to town. I'd discovered that I was emotionally and temperamentally unsuited to gambling on racehorses. It's too much of a strain on me, even when I'm on a dead cert.

"No thanks, Charlie. I'll give the races a miss if you don't mind."

THE LIZARD-SKINNER

I N THE EARLY sixties I was meat-hunting in South Westland, a shilling a pound for venison hung out at the road, and I got bored with it. I'd seen enough of snow and ice and rain and floods to last me for a while, so I decided to go to North Australia and have a go at crocodile shooting. I'd heard there was good money in the skins, a pound an inch. That made the skin of an eight-foot crocodile worth about a hundred quid and that was good money in those days.

I crossed the Tasman and bought a Land Rover and some basic camping gear and drove up through the middle of Australia and arrived at Burketown in the Gulf of Carpentaria at the same time as a crocodile-hunting rush was on. *The Australian Post* had featured an article about croc shooting and the big money to be made from the skins. They'd made it sound easy and hundreds of would-be croc hunters were pouring into the towns of the north.

The average bunch of these aspiring hunters consisted of two or three blokes with big hats and smooth-soled boots in a Holden ute towing a trailer with an aluminium dingy, outboard motor, tentage, tucker, spotlights, rifles, water bags, snake-bite kits and blow-up mattresses. They'd pull up outside the pub and go in and order a beer and casually ask the barman where all the crocodiles were.

"In the river," they'd be told, so they'd set up their camp right on the river bank and that night they'd go charging up and down the river in their motor boat, waving spotlights around that could be seen for a mile, searching for a crocodile that had probably heard them leave Sydney.

These men had come to pit themselves against the big salt-water crocodile but much smaller man-eaters very quickly drove them from the battle. The mosquitoes and sandflies in those mangrove swamps were fair little tinkers. Even in the daytime every bit of exposed skin would be black with mosquitoes. There were hordes of them, all insanely voracious and suicidal. You moved around in a cloud of them. You couldn't rig up your mosquito net without getting a few of them inside it. You'd suffer hours of discomfort before you'd open your net and go out amongst those mossies.

You'd see a bunch of croc shooters head off up the Eichardt River into endless miles of mangrove waterways in their sleeveless shirts, and you'd know they'd be back out of there very soon after their insect repellent ran out, and that never takes very long in places like that.

The mosquitoes in the swamps were wicked, but the sandflies everywhere else were diabolical. The North Australian sandfly is the nastiest insect I know of. It's a tiny grey speck like a fleck of cigarette ash, so small it can go through your mosquito net. It'll even get inside your swag. You don't see it and you don't feel it bite, you just suddenly come up in big white maddeningly-itchy lumps that'll turn into tropical ulcers if you scratch them too much.

Every campsite is on the highest, most exposed spot around so that any wind will blow the sandflies away. Every hut that's lived in is filled with putrid smoke from an old camp-oven full of smouldering camel or buffalo dung, to keep the sandflies away. The Aborigines smear themselves with dugong fat and put up with the smell and the flies crawling all over their faces in preference to those sandflies.

There'd been no mention of the sandfly in *The Australian*

Post article and yet it played a very large part in quickly sorting the men from the boys and sending all those croc shooters back to where they came from. I never subsequently met anybody who stuck it out from that kind of introduction to croc shooting. There was a lot of cheap croc gear going for a while there, but I didn't know what was of any actual use so I didn't buy any of it.

I hung around the far north for a few weeks, picking up what information I could about croc shooting, which wasn't much, until by chance I ran into a real croc-shooter, Harry Blumenthals, a Latvian, a loner, a real bushman and a genuine lizard-skinner. He'd been doing it for a living for ten years and had a muscle torn out of his arm by a crocodile. We got on well with each other from the start and after a couple of days in the pub we took off on a croc-shooting trip up the Robinson River. I learnt the basics of the game from the stern seat of Harry's little plywood dinghy.

No outboard motors for Harry, he paddled the dinghy from the front with a big Aborigine paddle. He paddled so quietly that his paddle didn't even dribble onto the surface when he lifted it out of the water. He wore a small six-volt spotlight on his forehead powered by torch batteries, because that's all you need to strike red sparks from the eyes of any crocodiles that are around.

When the eyes of a croc glow in his light Harry slides the dinghy so noiselessly towards it that the croc in the light can't tell how close he is. As he glides up to the square head and ridged snout of the big salty lying in the water under over-hanging trees Harry carefully lays his paddle on the sacks folded on the seat and picks up the twelve-foot harpoon pole lying along the gunwale, stands up and drives the barbed quill into the croc's scaled neck and pulls the pole off the quill in the same stabbing movement. The croc disappears with a slash and

115

Harry quickly puts the harpoon pole back on the gunwale and picks up the paddle and back-paddles to keep the dingy nose-on to the nylon rope attached to the quill looping out over the bow.

The rope stops running out. Harry puts down the paddle and picks up his fully-wooded .303 rifle and slides a bullet into the breech, sweeping the silent river with his light.

Ten minutes go by.

Fifteen minutes. He has to come up for air.

Twenty minutes.

Suddenly the eyes are gleaming in the light forty feet away out in the middle of the river. The thick silence is shattered by the blast of Harry's rifle and in its echoes the screaming of startled cockatoos in the trees along the riverbank. The white belly of the big croc rolls into the light and it is already beginning to sink by the time Harry paddles across to it. He loops the rope around the croc's jaw in three half-hitches and, holding the croc to the surface, chops it through the back of the neck with his axe to sever the spine.

"Got you," he mutters, putting the axe back under the seat.

He ties the croc to the dinghy and paddles towards the riverbank until he can get his rope around the branch of a tree. Hauling on the rope he snigs the croc as far up the bank as he can get it and ties it there to be skinned the next day and the skin packed away in salt in a sack. The skin was worth a pound an inch, as I'd been told, but across the belly and not its full length. It was still good money if you could get enough of them.

The reason why Harry harpooned the big crocs was because they swallow rocks so they sink effortlessly when they stop swimming. Makes it easy for them to sneak up on the pig or the wallaby or the cattle beast or the person. If you just shoot him he's liable to sink out of reach before you can get a rope on him. There's also the danger that the croc might only be stunned, they very often are, and if one of the big ones jack-knifed on you it'd fling you and your dinghy right out of the water. Harpooning them from the front is the surest and safest way of getting them.

I'd been intending to get a bit of gear and go off on my own once I'd learnt a bit about it but Harry and I worked together so well that we teamed up and hunted the rivers, the lagoons and the tidal estuaries of the Gulf of Carpenteria, from Cape York Peninsula to Arnhem Land. We got hundreds of croc skins and made good money.

Skinning was the hardest and trickiest part of it. The skin had to be knifed off every inch of the way and every knife-cut into the skin cost us a quid. There were times when I'd have believed it was easier to skin a crowbar than a big croc. They were so heavy we had to work on them in the water so we could move them around. Sandfly country. Sandflies can always tell when you've got both hands busy.

We got several real big crocs, one-and-a-half-ton eighteen-footers. Harpooning one of those from a cockleshell dingy can be quite a thrill, but we never took unnecessary risks. If we didn't like the look of a situation, like the croc not having enough room to get away from us easily, we usually let him go and came back and had a go at him another time. The consequences of making a balls-up with a big croc made you real careful with him, but we still had the odd slip-up.

I was sitting with a rifle in a big paperbark tree hanging over a lagoon one day, waiting for a big croc we knew was in there to surface, and the branch I was perched on suddenly broke off and dumped me in the lagoon with him. That was a sensation, gave me a hell of a fright. I was out of that water before I was properly wet. We caught that croc in our barramundi net and retrieved the rifle with a shark hook on the end of the harpoon pole. Our only telescopic sight was ruined but somehow I didn't care too much about that.

Another time Harry had a much more serious encounter with a croc. He got in some quicksand between the river and a big croc he was sneaking up on, a fifteen-footer. He was stuck and the croc had seen him. The croc charged towards him and stopped about twenty feet away. Your chances of dropping a big croc with a rifle when he's head-on to you are incredibly slim, especially when you're up to your crutch in quicksand, but for reasons known only to whoever was in Harry's corner that day the croc turned away and he got a shot in at the side of its head, and his first bullet penetrated the thick rubbery skull and dropped the croc in its tracks. Most of the time your first shot won't do that with a croc that bulky.

Harry gave it another one to make sure and extracted himself from the quicksand, which he'd only been in for about fifteen seconds. He came back to camp to get me to come and give him a hand with the croc. He was still a bit shaky so I made him sit down with a brew of tea.

"He could have got me that time," Harry muttered into his pannikin.

That croc had been waiting there to grab any wallaby or pig or dingo, or anything else, before it could flounder its way through that patch of quicksand. We figured that the reason it hesitated to grab Harry was because he was unfamiliar and wasn't trying to run away. In nature everything runs away from a fifteen-foot croc and Harry's behaviour must have confused it.

Notwithstanding these sorts of incidents, the crocodiles gave us less trouble than those North Australian mosquitoes and sandflies. Our only protection from them was long pants, long sleeves and plenty of insect repellent, and still we were constantly bitten and itching.

After sharing these and many other adventures for more than a year Harry and I split up. He wanted a break from croc shooting and I didn't blame him, he'd had a long unbroken spell of it and needed a change. If you got too bored with a thing like croc shooting you might start getting careless. Harry went to Mt Isa to work in the mines, and the last I heard of him he was living in an underground house, digging opal at Lightning Ridge. I'll always remember my mate Harry the Lizard-skinner with gratitude and affection. He taught me a lot and we had a lot of fun together. Thanks mate.

I hunted crocs on my own for another year after that and then went over to Cairns, where I bought a lugger with my croc-skin money and spent a year grooving up and down the Great Barrier Reef, fishing, diving, beachcombing, croc-shooting and generally having a good time, until I was shipwrecked and marooned on an island and rescued and taken to New Guinea, from where I made my way back to New Zealand and acted a part in one of our early feature films, but that's another yarn.

THE WAYFARER

WE ALL KNOW the type of person I shall politely refer to here as the 'Wayfarer'. There's one in just about every group, gang, gathering or agglomeration of people. They're usually tolerated, and carried through each situation by those of us not afflicted with whatever causes Wayfever. We don't like to believe that there's as many Wayfarers around us as there are, but the sad fact is that wherever there's a bunch of more than four people there's a strong likelihood that there'll be a Wayfarer among them.

I've run across my fair share of them in my time, they seem to pick on me, and I usually try to forget about them as soon as possible, but there's one who will always stand out in my memory as the perfect example of the Wayfarer.

I was shooting crocs out of Cooktown at the mouth of the Endeavour River at the time, and I'd been waiting around for a skin-cheque to arrive. Bert Hudson came in out of some weather in his hundred-foot boat, the *Malanda,* on his way from Cairns to Thursday Island at the tip of Australia, with twenty tons of gelignite. It wasn't much of a cargo but if you carried explosives you weren't allowed to carry anything else.

Bert was a bit off-colour and got a lift up to the hospital in Jack Stewart's truck, where they decided that his appendix had to come out. The next day Frank the Abo came down to the wharf where I had my thirty-footer, the *Waterwitch,* tied up, and said that Bert wanted to see me urgently. I went up to the hospital, where Bert was propped up in bed looking a bit under the weather.

"I'll have to get you to take that cargo up to T.I. for me, Crumpy," he said. "You're the only one I can trust the boat with. I've lost two days as it is and if I don't get that gelignite there by Friday I could lose the contract."

"Not a problem, Bert," I said. "The weather's settling down. I'll get away this afternoon."

"Thanks mate," he said. "The boat's all ready. My brother-in-law, Claud, is on board. He'll give you a hand. He's never been to sea before, he's a shopkeeper, but he's a good bloke."

And that's how I came to run into the most useless, blithering, once-in-a-lifetime Wayfarer I ever met.

I didn't have a Skipper's Ticket but I could handle Bert's boat okay. I'd been on a few trips with him, taking loads of fuel and other cargo up to Weipa and places like that. We used to anchor in the river mouth and roll the drums of diesel over the side and the Abos would swim them ashore and roll them up the beach. We lowered the sacks of flour and other stuff into their dugout canoes with the boat's winch.

Anyway, we slipped our moorings and we weren't out of the Endeavour River before I began to discover what a useless coot brother-in-law Claud was. He called the hatches lids. He didn't know starboard from port, the bow from the stern, the helm from the hatchway. He couldn't tie a knot, cook a feed, read a chart or steer a course. And he couldn't learn, he was a Wayfarer.

It was fairly plain sailing. There's a stretch of open water between the Great Barrier Reef and the mainland all the way up the Cape York Peninsula to Thursday Island, with a few islets and sand-cays to watch out for. I got brother-in-law Claud up in the wheel-house and tried to show him on the chart where we had to go, but he was never going to get the message, so I showed him our present course on the compass and put him on the wheel.

He was hopeless. He kept over-correcting, our wake was like the tracks of a drunken snake. I pointed out Cape Flattery and told him to steer straight for that, but he started steering round it when it was still five miles away and ended up heading out towards the Reef, weaving all over the sea. I took the helm and told him to go down to the galley and cook something to eat. He came back up to the wheel-house to ask me what he should cook. Then he came back to ask how to make the stove go.

"You turn the bloody thing on and light it," I told him.

This was just lovely. I had many long hours at the wheel ahead of me. After about an hour I smelt something burning and left the wheel-house and went below to see what Claud was up to. The cabin was full of smoke. He'd burnt a pot full of baked beans and set fire to a tea towel. He reckoned he was taking sea-sick pills that were making him inattentive.

I got the mess sorted out and went up and put us back on course and then lowered the trailing-booms that came down from the mast and held the bowden cable and piano wire trailing lines out from the boat.

It wasn't long before I hooked a nice big turrum, and by running between the wheel-house and the deck I boated the fish, filleted it, chopped it up and marinated it in a bowl of vinegar and chopped onion and kept it in the wheel-house. That's all I had to eat all the way up to T.I.

Claud came up to ask me what he should do next.

"Nothing," I told him. "Absolutely nothing. Don't touch anything. Here, have some of this raw fish."

He took one look at it and gulped and gurgled, mumbled something about feeling a little squeamish, and vanished below deck and stayed there.

We arrived at Thursday Island in the early dawn, thirty-eight hours at a constant twelve knots. After berthing at the wharf I got a couple of hours' kip before having to go on deck to supervise unloading the cargo. I got it signed for, took on fuel, went up town and had a feed of steak and eggs and discovered the other thing that Claud was good at. I already knew he could sleep, he'd slept most of the way up here. Now I found that he was also pretty good at eating. He put away a huge feed, which I had to pay for. He had no money.

Claud went back to the boat for a rest. I had a few beers in the pub with a couple of fishermen I knew and then went on board and slept all night. We set off back down the coast the next morning. The weather was holding and I stuck out the trailing lines and caught six big Spanish mackerel. A bit of pocket money.

That night it was calm, cloudless and moonless. The stars were as bright as it only gets in the tropics. You could almost read by their light. By the time we were passing Princess Charlotte Bay the hours at the wheel were getting to me. I was having trouble keeping my eyes open. We still had about thirteen hours of steaming ahead of us. I'd pulled in the lines but the trailing-booms were still out, and I'd found that keeping the tip of one of the booms on the Southern Cross kept us on course. There was at least three hours of open going ahead. I went below and woke Claud and got him up in the wheel-house.

"You see those four stars there?" I said, pointing them out to him.

"Those ones?" he said.

"Yes, those ones. That's the Southern Cross. All you have to do is keep the tip of that trailing boom on those stars. Do you think you can do that?"

"I'll try," he said.

"Well try then," I said, handing over the wheel.

He over-steered something terrible but he seemed to have the idea of what he was supposed to do. I watched him for a while and then stumbled below and fell into a bunk and flaked out.

I don't know how long I was asleep but I woke instantly, as you only ever do on a boat when you sense that something's wrong. She was moving wrong in the swells.

I sprang up and looked out a porthole. There was reef all around us, you could see the phosphorus in the water creaming on coral. I bolted up to the wheel-house and shoved Claud out of the way and brought her round. We'd been heading straight into the Barrier Reef. I throttled her right back and eased her through a twisting passage of black water until we were out into open going again. We bumped once or twice but not seriously. I was shaking. It had been a close call.

"What's the matter?" said Claud. He couldn't see what all the fuss was about.

"You are, you useless bastard!" I shouted at him. "Why the bloody hell didn't you keep the tip of that trailing boom on those stars like I told you?"

"Stars? Oh them," he said. "We went past those away back there. They're miles behind us now."

What can you say? He really believed he'd overtaken the stars. A Wayfarer!

"Go away," I told him (or words to that effect). "I don't want to see you on deck again until we get there."

I was wide awake and shaken. I brought her up to fourteen knots, arrived at Cooktown in the afternoon and had to wait a couple of hours for the tide and took her in over the bar and berthed at the wharf, real glad to be there. I didn't speak to brother-in-law Claud again. Couldn't trust myself.

I went up to the hospital, where Bert was hobbling around in a dressing gown.

"How did it go, Crumpy?"

"Not a problem, Bert," I said.

"How was Claud? He's a good bloke isn't he?"

"Sure, Bert. He's a grand bunch of chaps all right."

What can you say? Brother-in-law Claud had driven the boat right past the Southern Cross, and come within inches of putting us up on the reef, a hundred and fifty miles from the nearest help. A Wayfarer from way back!

GARTH

I'VE SEEN AND heard of some unusual pets in my time, but by far the most unusual one I ever ran into was Garth. It happened in the sixties. My wife and I were tin-scratching at Mt Poverty in Helenvale, north Queensland, and it was there that we inherited Garth. We'd moved into a corrugated-iron hut among trees on the bank of the Endeavour River and worked from there, diverting water and running the tin-bearing material over riffles and collecting the black grains of tin. Thirty quid a bagful. You could make a living if you worked hard, and a profit if you were lucky as well.

The previous occupant of the hut was a bloke called 'The Arab'. He'd taken his entire menagerie with him when he'd left but after two weeks he came back with Garth in a zipped-up bag. Garth wouldn't settle in The Arab's new camp out on the saltbush plain. He'd become listless and sulky, not eating, staying home curled up on his bunk all night and generally making it plain that he was fretting for the cool water, rocks and bush of Mt Poverty.

Garth was ten, The Arab told us, and he'd had him since he was seven. We thought he was talking about Garth's age, but he meant his length in feet. You see, The Arab was a snake lover and Garth was a ten-foot diamond-back rock python. He liked people, The Arab assured us, and was completely harmless. He ate mice and rats and frogs and scraps and any kind of bird or egg. He liked a feed of fish or mince or a wallaby leg whenever he could get it. He preferred to eat in the mornings and then curl up on his sacking bunk in the shade of the hut porch all day. At night he usually went off hunting and came into the hut for any scraps at breakfast time. He loved coming for a swim with you in the river and having his neck stroked behind his head.

Unlike The Arab, my wife and I weren't all that keen on snakes. We'd always given them a wide berth. The idea of having one hanging around the camp like a pet didn't appeal to us.

"Why don't you just take it somewhere and let it go?" we wanted to know.

"Wouldn't be any use," he said. "This is his stamping ground. He'd just come right back here. They're very territorial."

We finally had to agree and Garth was unzipped and tipped out of his bag. Black, yellow and bronze coils of him glistening in the sunlight. Flat diamond-shaped head with yellow slitted eyes and forked tongue darting in and out. He unrolled himself and slithered along the porch and up onto his bunk and made a big production of curling himself up in the middle of it. He was home, and he didn't look all that harmless to us. Well, I thought, we can always knock him off if he gets to be too much of a nuisance.

Garth settled in with us as though he'd been ours all the time. He had his routine and didn't like it being disrupted, but the worst thing about him was his appearance. It took a bit of getting used to. It's a bit disconcerting having a dirty big snake come sliding into the hut and put its head on your leg and ask for the rest of your mutton sandwich with its tongue.

He'd have you on, too. He'd come in from hunting all night and beg food off you as though he was starving, and his belly would be bulging like a stocking with a loaf of bread in it. He was sneaky as well, food vanished in the most mysterious ways. He had an uncanny knack of knowing when you weren't watching the chops or sausages you were preparing to cook.

You'd turn back to them and they'd be gone and Garth's tail would be disappearing out the door.

He had some rather un-snakelike tastes, Garth. He'd eat the dishcloth, he ate a sneaker, he loved a pound of butter, he flogged my packet of tobacco off the arm of the chair I was sitting in and I only just got it back off him before he swallowed it. He'd grab something and take off with it and if you could get him by the tail and hang on he'd drop it, once he knew he was caught. He was usually philosophical about miss-outs and within a few minutes he'd be back inside, flicking his tongue around and eyeing up anything you had in your hand. He even snatched a saveloy off my fork as I was raising it to my mouth.

We had a Garth-proof cupboard but heaven help us if we ever left it open. Everything had to be kept shut in the cupboard or in tins. We never saw any rats or mice around the place, but Garth was worse than a plague of them when it came to keeping your food safe. Even the old trick of hanging food from the rafters was no good with him around. He could climb like a supercharged rata vine.

We found one way of partly controlling Garth: he was scared of fire. We didn't need a very big cooking fire in that climate but Garth wouldn't go anywhere near it. If we wanted to protect something from him we only had to put it beside the fire, but we couldn't do that with things like butter and Garth particularly liked butter. Whenever we brought a pound of butter out he'd fix his eyes on it until he either got a chance to grab it or it was put away again. He got away with a lot of our butter until we got the idea of lighting a candle, even in the daytime, and leaving it beside the butter. Garth was so scared of fire that he'd recoil and shrink away if you held even a candle too close to him. And if you wanted to call him you only had to go outside and start scraping a plate and if Garth was anywhere around he'd come slithering along to see what you had for him this time. That was about the only degree of control we had over him.

Now you mightn't know this, we didn't, but rock pythons will get as cheeky as you let them, and my wife started spoiling Garth rotten. She talked to him as though he was a child, she called him Diddums, she bought meat off the butcher for him when we went to town for supplies, she put a special blanket on his bed, instead of giving him a kick she'd step over him or around him, and a ten-foot snake in a twenty-foot by fifteen-foot hut takes up a lot of space.

My wife didn't take any notice of me when I warned her we were overdoing it. Garth was becoming over-familiar. He wasn't begging any more, he was demanding, and if he didn't get what he wanted he'd go all moody and slither away and climb up into the mango tree and drape himself over a branch and sulk.

He followed us half a mile to work one day and ate our lunch that was hanging in a bag in a tree. We knew it was Garth because he'd thrown a wobbly when we wouldn't let him have the omelette we'd cooked for our breakfast that morning, and even the newspaper our lunch had been wrapped in was gone. Garth didn't mind a bit of newspaper as long as it was wrapped around something he liked. He soon forgave us, though, and by the time we got back to the hut that night things were back to normal. Mr Bulgebelly was innocently curled up on his bunk and pretended to wake up just as we were dishing up our meal.

He tried to swipe a sausage off my plate one night and I gave him a whack with the broom, and he backed away with a hurt look and sulked across to his mother, who called him a poor Diddums and gave him a sausage off her plate. He had her conned.

When Garth wanted something he'd give you a smoodge by wrapping a coil of himself around your leg and giving you an affectionate squeeze, and there was a surprising amount of strength in one of Garth's smoodges. He playfully wrapped himself around my wife's waist when we were swimming in the river with him one day and just about drowned her before I could get him unwrapped.

Another drawback, we found, to having a python for a pet was the reactions of visitors to him. People are funny about snakes. One day a young bloke who'd dropped a roll of wire off at the hut for us came tearing down to where we were working to breathlessly warn us that there was a huge poisonous snake on our porch. When an English hitchhiker we'd offered a bunk for the night suddenly started screaming we knew it was only because she'd just spotted Garth sliding along the rafter of the hut in the candle light. The tin-buyer ran back to his truck to get his gun. A cousin of my wife who came on a visit just about had a nervous breakdown and left after three days. She said Garth gave her the creeps.

It was incidents like this that lead us to the discovery of the most efficient deterrent to visitors we ever found. We nailed a sheet of corrugated iron on a gum tree where the track to the hut came off the road and painted a big sign on it saying,

THE SNAKE IS TAME

That cut the number of our visitors from very few to none at all. Quite a few times we heard vehicles pull up out on the road, pause long enough to read the sign and think about it for a few moments, and then drive away again.

Garth was dominating our scene more than I felt was right. We found ourselves always defending him. We'd run into someone we knew in town and they'd say, "Have you still got that snake out there?"

"Yes. Why?" we'd say.

"What are you going to do with it?" they'd say.

A good question. I didn't have any answers to it and my

wife didn't want any, she still reckoned that Garth was being misunderstood. Meanwhile, the object of all this continued chucking his growing weight around us as though he owned the place. My wife said it was just because he was a typical male, which turned out to be a bit of a joke between us later on.

With the passage of time and tribulation even my wife had to admit that Garth, cute and interesting and all as he was, was more trouble than he was worth. We could never relax whether he was around or not, and we were stuck with him. We began to wonder what on earth we were going to do with him, but Garth's fate was settled in the way most fates are, by coincidence. Some people in a boat coming down the river saw the smoke from our fire and came ashore for a look. They were a middle-aged German couple and two Abo blokes. We invited them up to the hut for a pannikin of tea, where the German bloke took some photographs of us tin-scratchers. We'd been doing it for four months.

I thought to tell them we had a tame snake lurking around somewhere but someone was talking at the time and I missed the chance. Garth had a habit of disappearing when visitors arrived and turning up again when the food came out. We liked to warn people about him, the arrival of a ten-foot python can play merry hell with a tea party.

We were sitting on the hut porch drinking tea and eating damper and wild turkey when the German woman suddenly said, "Oh, what a lovely diamond-back! Where did you get her?"

Garth had come pouring himself around the corner of the hut, flickering his tongue and waving his head towards anyone who looked as though they might like to share their food with him.

"Did you say her?" my wife said.

"Yes," said the woman. "You can tell by their markings. The pattern on the male is larger and bolder. This is a marvellous female specimen."

She started stroking Garth behind the head and letting him get too close to her leg of plain-turkey. He liked a bit of turkey. My wife and I looked at each other. Garth was a lady snake!

The German woman was a herpetologist (we didn't know what it meant either – it's someone who mucks around with snakes). She showed us a permit she had from the Queensland government to catch certain types of snakes to supply to zoos. They had two taipans, a king-brown and two black water snakes in boxes in their boat. Garth held no terrors for them, they made a great fuss of him and he lapped it up. He lay coiled untidily at the herpetologist's feet with a coil around her leg and his head on her lap, deigning to accept the stroking and all the turkey that was left in the camp oven.

My wife and I never did adjust to the idea of Garth being a female. The herpetologist told us a whole lot of stuff about the diamond-back rock python but we could have added a fair bit to what she knew. We lived with one of them.

Well, you guessed it, the herpetologist wanted Garth. How much money did we want for her? She would be put in a perfect rock-python environment and looked after for the rest of her life, much safer than out here in the wild.

My wife and I went for a walk and had a yarn about it. The wet season was coming on and we were going to have to move back onto our boat, and there was no way we could take Garth with us. We knew too many people who'd be inclined to deal to Garth if they found him hanging around. He was too unafraid of humans. So we let Garth go with the herpetologist. We put him in a hessian sack and the two Abo blokes carried him down to the boat on a pole and that was the last we saw of him.

We missed Garth around the place for a while, but agreed that he was probably pretty contented in the zoo. He always preferred to have food dished up to him than go out and hunt for it.

Yep, they make an interesting pet all right, the old rock-python, but I wouldn't recommend rushing out and getting yourself one. They can get too interesting.

Rum Jungle Jim

I FIRST CROSSED paths with Rum Jungle Jim McKenzie in the bar of Jimmy Adams' pub in Cooktown on the Great Barrier Reef. He was an interesting-looking bloke. His face was leathery and creased from years of exposure to the tropical sun and wind, and the hand wrapped around his glass of square gin was gnarled and scarred from years of hard work and arthritis. He was bare-footed and wore a pair of baggy shorts and a singlet and had an out-of-shape straw hat perched on his head. The hair on his head and chest was long and white. He was chasing seventy and living on the pension in a small empty shop down by the waterfront.

I got to know Jungle Jim and spent many hours enjoying his yarns about life spent on the Seven Seas, and around the coasts of Australia and the islands of the Pacific. He'd been a Pom originally and still had an old-fashioned courtesy about him, which was unusual for someone who'd lived the kind of life he had. They're usually as rough as guts, those blokes.

Jungle Jim had run away to sea in 1907 at the age of fourteen and served before the mast on sailing ships, cargo boats and whalers. He'd sailed with men who'd manned the slave trading ships. He'd ended up in the South Seas forty years before and never got away. He'd successfully made the big change from sail to motor-powered boats, but still talked nostalgically about the sailing ships, and like a lot of those old sailors Jungle Jim was a bit superstitious. Didn't approve of women on board a boat, some boats were self-destructive and had to be carefully watched, never expect more than three days of fair weather, don't cross the Tropic of Capricorn on a Friday, never put to sea with three different nationalities on board and so on. He had some lurid tales about things that had happened to people who'd sailed against the rules.

Jungle Jim had sailed with the notorious Errol Flynn and told me how Flynn had sold a copper mine in Papua to two blokes. He put them ashore at the mine from his yacht and then sailed away with all their supplies. A few months later the two blokes caught up with Flynn in a bar in Port Moresby and demanded to be paid for the stuff he'd swiped off them. Flynn was broke and suggested that they take it out of his hide, so they did, only Flynn cleaned up the both of them and finished his drink and sauntered out of there. Jungle Jim wouldn't sail with him after he heard about that and Flynn's schooner went up on the reef. Jungle Jim reckoned that the two things were definitely connected. Flynn had gone against the unwritten laws of seamanship.

Jungle Jim had ridden out cyclones in sailing ships and indulged in a bit of smuggling and trading copra and other such activities. He'd once done a year in Fanny Bay jail for bringing twelve illegal Timorese immigrants into Darwin. They'd taken a battering in the Straits and the old wooden yacht Jungle Jim was supposed to be delivering for a firm in Darwin sprung a couple of planks and they only just kept her afloat long enough to limp into Darwin Harbour. She went down a quarter of a mile off the beach and Jungle Jim and his twelve illegal immigrants came ashore in a six-foot dinghy and clinging to a couple of floats. This performance attracted the attention of the Customs Officers and they were all arrested. The Timorese were deported back to where they'd come from and Jungle Jim served most of his sentence in the pub across the road from the jail.

Jungle Jim and I became cronies and whenever I was in

port we usually had a session or two. Then one night in the cabin of my boat tied up at the Cooktown wharf, when we'd given a bottle of square gin a decent nudge, Jungle Jim revealed to me that he was afflicted. He'd done a terrible thing once that had haunted him ever since. He'd never told anyone about it before and swore me to secrecy for fear that they could still get him for it. Jim's dead just now and I don't think he'd mind me sharing his story with you. It's a hell of a yarn.

Rum Jungle Jim was skippering a sixty-foot gaff-rigged pearling lugger in the Timor Sea, with a crew of six Japanese divers, diving for trochus shell. There was no motor in the boat, they depended entirely on sail. Jim slept in a small deck cabin and the divers slept on small wooden platforms laid on top of the shell in the hold. They cooked over a fire in a drum on the deck and lived mainly on rice and trochus boiled in salt water.

Knowing Jim it was easy to see how the situation developed. He was one of nature's gentlemen and not geared up for bossing other men around. The Second World War was brewing and there was hostility creeping in between the Japanese and the Australians. Jim's crew were openly making maps of the Australian coast.

They were becalmed in the Gulf of Carpentaria, twelve miles off Mornington Island, when it came to a head. They'd been there for three days. It was sweltering hot, a hundred degrees in the waterbag. The crew were getting more and more arrogant and disobedient. Pretending not to understand him, ignoring his orders to conserve water, fighting among themselves, refusing to man the bilge pump. Jim was getting worried about the situation.

On the third day he looked out of his cabin and saw one of the Japanese divers being shaved by one of the others. He had the Australian flag around his shoulders.

"Get that flag off that man please," said Jim.

136

The diver wiped soap off his face with the flag and stared defiantly at Jim. This was open confrontation. If Jim couldn't stop it right then he was going to wind up over the side with his throat cut. Lost at sea. The only firearm on the boat was a rusty old .44 lever-action saddle carbine he sometimes used for scaring away the sharks when the divers came up with the baskets of shell. He reached into the cabin and got the gun and jacked a bullet into the breech and aimed at the diver with the flag.

"Get that flag off please," he repeated.

The diver arrogantly continued wiping his face with the flag. Jim aimed a foot above his head and fired to scare him, and the bullet hit the diver in the middle of his forehead and blew his brains out the back of his head. He flew over backwards and lay sprawled on the deck.

Jim was shocked and stood there looking at the gun in his hands. The other divers all started bowing and begging. They got the flag off the dead diver and came bowing up to Jim with it. There were brains and blood on it.

"What we do now, Cap'n?" they asked.

"Put that dead man in the longboat and row him to the leper colony on Mornington and get them to radio the police in Darwin and tell them what happened," he said.

They scurried to do what he ordered and even washed down the deck without having to be told. This Cap'n was not to be mucked around with. He shoots a man through the head in cold blood for disobeying him and then sends the body to the authorities. What magnificent flair! This was their kind of Cap'n! Shogun!

Jim was sitting in his cabin wondering what the hell when he heard the longboat come back alongside. They'd only been gone half an hour. The divers seriously and regretfully reported that they'd been washing the dead man over the side of the boat and the sharks took him. And that's what Jim wrote in the log book. Taken by sharks. Not an unusual entry in a log book in those times.

He had no more trouble with his crew after that and Rum Jungle Jim became known and respected among the divers throughout the region as one of the fairest but toughest skippers afloat. They were proud to sail with him and he never had any trouble getting a good crew together after that. He could take his pick of them.

But the incident had affected him. He couldn't keep the memory of it out of his head. All these years later, with the veils of distraction dissolved by schnapps, the vision of brains and blood came to him as vividly as when it happened. He was haunted by it. He couldn't even be sure whether it had actually been an accident or whether he'd subconsciously meant to do it.

I tried to point out to him that as the Captain he was probably within his rights to do whatever was necessary to quell a mutiny, and it was an accident anyway, but Jungle Jim wasn't parting with his affliction that easily. He wasn't even listening to me. As a leper clings to his leprosy, Rum Jungle Jim clung possessively to his burden of torment. He was too much of a gentleman to be able to shrug it off, that would have made him feel worse about it.

He sculled his glass of square gin and stared into the candle on the table between us and shook his head and muttered, "I wouldn't have thought the gun was shooting so far out at that range."

We slept on board that night and Rum Jungle Jim called out to someone in his sleep to secure that sheet and bring her about please. Steady now! He was out at sea again with the wind blowing in his hair, feeling her heel over as he tacked her through a passage in the reef. I hoped he wouldn't get to the part where he was becalmed in the gulf with a crew of mutinous Japanese divers on board.

As I mentioned, my old mate Rum Jungle Jim Mckenzie hoisted his mains'l and sailed off, still haunted, into the Great Beyond some years ago now, and I feel confident that he's at last been relieved of his affliction. Hell of a thing to live with though.

SAFARI IN GHUZNEE STREET

IN THE MID-SIXTIES I acted a small part in an early New Zealand movie, called *Runaway*. I even remember a bit of the dialogue from that film:

LEADING MAN: *"Is this your hut?"*

CRUMP: (eyeing up the leading lady and chewing on a hunk of meat) *"Nothin' belongs to no one around here, mate."*

Anyway, when the filming was over the producer and director approached me about making a film based on a book I'd written about hunting crocodiles in the Gulf of Carpentaria. I thought it was a good idea and the producer and director flew off to Normanton in North Queensland to check out locations, leaving me to work out the slight problem of getting actors to work around live crocodiles without getting themselves killed.

You can't tame saltwater crocodiles. There had recently been a news item about a keeper at the Brisbane zoo who'd fed and looked after a fourteen-foot salty for twelve years. He'd got a bit too close to it one day and it'd taken to him and killed him. We didn't want that happening to our actors. I knew how to catch crocs, but as for letting anyone near them – that was going to take a bit of working out.

I consulted a bunch of veterinary blokes who'd opened a clinic in Wellington, where I was shacked up in a small flat, about using one of those new-fangled tranquilliser guns and what sort of drugs you'd need to quieten down a crocodile. There was no information available on the subject, but they agreed to try and get me one of the guns, which would have to be imported, and work out what drugs and quantities would be worth experimenting with. That was about the best I could hope for.

In due course the gun arrived. It was called a Capture Gun and operated with a compressed CO_2 cartridge. You put the drug you wanted to use in a dart and pushed it up the barrel, closed it, flicked a catch on the side of the gun and fired it into the animal. The force of the impact released a chemical which then expanded, injecting the drug into the animal.

It wasn't a very efficient weapon. I practised with it on a cardboard box out on the lawn when the landlady was out. It had a very low velocity and a very curved trajectory. Forty yards was the maximum range it would carry with any accuracy and even at that distance you had to aim high.

One afternoon I was swotting up on some literature they'd given me about the effects of various drugs, dosages, body-weights and stuff. The phone rang. It was one of the vets from the clinic. A circus elephant had gone stroppy on them and escaped from the wharf and wandered up through the city. It was a valuable animal and they were going to have a go at tranquillising it. I had the only dart gun they knew of. Could I bring the gun and some darts down to Ghuznee Street as soon as possible.

Ghuznee Street was a narrow city street with quaint old houses jammed along each side and cars parked along the kerb. When I got there crowds of people were gathered in the roadway being kept back by police and traffic officers. A bunch of circus people and police and the vets were standing around a Land Rover in the middle of the road and a big cow elephant was in the street about sixty yards away.

If you'd never seen an elephant in your life you could see that this one was definitely het-up about something. Its ears were stiff and flapping, it was shaking its head and waving its trunk around. It had a short chain around one of its front feet with a two-foot iron spike hanging from it. There was a bloke there with a short pole that had a spike and a hook on the end of it, but I couldn't see what he was going to do with that. He wasn't even game to go near it.

As we watched the elephant ambled over to a parked car and shunted it with the front of its trunk. It lifted the car up on its two off-side wheels and then let it drop back down with a dented door and a broken window.

They said that the circus had been brought up from the West Coast that morning by train and the elephant had been reaching its trunk over the top of the cattle wagon it was in, and eating bunches of the tutu bushes that grew along the railway line, and poisoned itself. Whether that was right or not, it had certainly done something to itself. It was not a happy elephant.

One of the vets loaded one of my darts with two cc's of a drug called Trilafon, a powerful muscle-relaxant I'd been reading up on. It took us a few minutes to convince the police I was the only one who could use the gun accurately and they agreed to let me do the shooting. I had to go through a yard and get behind the houses, climb over a couple of fences and sneak into range of the elephant. You don't realise how big elephants actually are until you're sneaking up on a mad one with a toy gun in your hands. I have to confess that I was a bit nervous. I poked the barrel through a hedge and fired the dart into the elephant's rump at thirty yards. It gave a squeal when the dart stuck into it and shambled over to a car and shoved it up against the curb, leaving a big dent in the door. Then it stood there waving its trunk around and making elephant noises. I went back to where the vets were and we waited for the drug to take effect.

After about twenty minutes there was still no sign of the elephant settling down and one of the vets suggested that its

142

body weight was too much for the dosage we'd used, so they loaded another dart and I sneaked back and fired it into the elephant's other rump.

Within minutes of my having darted it with the second dose the first one began to work. The elephant started to droop, standing, swaying and nodding. Then one of the vets arrived back from somewhere and said he'd just found out that elephants have a highly developed nervous system and are very sensitive to drugs. This was a bit of a worry.

After a while the bloke with the pole carefully went up and gave the elephant a prod with it. It hardly responded. We'd quietened it down all right, but the problem now was that we might have quietened it down too much. An overdose of muscle-relaxant could relax its heart muscles and kill it. One of the vets shot off to try to dig up some kind of antidote and it was decided to try to get the elephant back down to the wharf before it collapsed in the roadway.

We prodded and pushed the going-to-sleep elephant down Ghuznee Street and into Taranaki Street, heaving one leg a step forward and then another. By this time everyone was knocking off work and it was a major disruption, directing the traffic away from our scene of operations. The police were kept busy keeping the crowds of people clear of us.

By the time we'd got our elephant down to Manners Street it was starting to buckle at the knees. The vets had given it a shot of some stimulant but it was impossible to tell if it was making any difference. The elephant nearly went down in the middle of Jervois Quay and only just regained its balance. We just got it to the gates of Taranaki Wharf. It went down on its front knees and then its back legs gave way and it squatted there with its trunk doubled up under its dropped head.

I went home after that, taking my tranquilliser gun and darts with me. They weren't going to need them any more. The vets worked on the elephant through the night and managed to keep it alive. A couple of days later there was a photograph of it in the paper, placidly eating hay with the bloke with the pole sitting on its neck.

The publicity was no doubt good for the circus but it didn't do me much good. They came and confiscated my tranquilliser gun and darts. It appeared I wasn't legally allowed to have them because I wasn't qualified to use the drugs.

The filming project fell through from lack of finance and all I was left with was the memory of the adventure. After all, it isn't every day a bloke gets to shoot an elephant in the middle of Wellington, even though it was only with a tranquilliser gun.

SPONDYLATING LEPTOSPIROSIS

IN THE FIFTIES a mate of mine who was going overseas offered me the use of his flat in Christchurch for three months. That suited me fine, I needed to come in off the road for a spell. I saw my mate off at the airport and settled into his flat to be a city slicker for a while.

My mate had said that a relative of his called Angus was coming up from Dunedin and might stay in the flat for a day or two until he could get somewhere to live. That was okay with me and when Angus arrived I made him welcome and he moved into the other room with his one small suitcase and began to create one of the worst messes I've ever seen a room get in.

He was an unusual sort of a bloke, Angus. It wasn't easy to work out what he did for a living, he was very vague about it. He was likeable enough but there was something I couldn't figure out about him. He told me he got a small medical benefit every month because of a rare incurable disease he suffered from called spondylating leptospirosis, which prevented him from doing any physical work. I raised an eyebrow at that, but he protested that it was fair dinkum. He reckoned it was a disease you got from pigs and it affected your spine. Sounded like a good one to me, but if he was getting away with it. . .

Whether it was the spondylating leptospirosis or not I don't know, but Angus certainly didn't do any physical work in the four or five years I knew him. He did plenty of non-physical stuff but it took a while to figure out exactly what it was. He seemed to make his living out of the newspapers. He'd get up in the morning and go down to the dairy and get the morning paper and bring it back and throw the main part of it on the floor and sit at the table, chain-smoking cigarettes and chain-drinking cups of tea, while he went through the classified ads and public notices, marking the items he was interested in with a pencil he sharpened onto the floor with the bread knife. Once he'd edited out what he wanted he mutilated the paper further by tearing it out. Then he'd straighten his tie crooked and go off to do whatever it was he did all day, leaving his paper scattered all over the kitchen.

At night he'd come home with the evening paper and give it the same treatment. Within a week I had to point out to Angus that the flat was filling up with all the newspaper he was chucking everywhere. No trouble to Angus, he apologised and gathered up the newspaper in armfuls and threw it into his room and shut the door on it.

In another week his room was knee-deep in crumpled sheets of newspaper. I told him I was worried about him smoking in there with all that loose paper lying around. No trouble to Angus, he kicked all the paper into a corner of the room and trampled it partly flat. I asked him why he didn't just stuff it into rubbish bags and get rid of it. I even offered to give him a hand with it, but his spondylating leptospirosis was playing up on him and he never got around to it.

Angus never washed his socks, underpants, singlets or shirts; when they got too dirty he bought new ones, and the old clothes and the wrappings from the new ones were all mixed up with the newspaper, which filled half his room to the height of the windowsill by the time a bunch of us attacked it and filled eleven rubbish bags with it and took it to the tip.

Apart from this and a few other eccentricities I got to like Angus, who seemed to have settled into the flat for as long as he was going to get away with it. I discovered that he had a

146

remarkable knowledge of what everything was worth, whether it was a house, a horse, a car, a boat or a bottle opener. Whatever you wanted to buy Angus could save you money on it by knowing where to get it at the best price. I had him sussed, he was a wheeler and dealer in the city, and he'd often buy stuff at auctions and sell it at a profit without even having to handle it.

I found out what a terrific salesman Angus was when we had a visit from the landlord and discovered the arrangements our mate had made for his rent to be paid weren't working. It was seventy quid in arrears and if we didn't come up with the money by the end of the week we were out on the street. That gave us three days. Neither of us had anything like that much money but Angus said he thought he knew how we could get it. Not having any ideas of my own I placed myself in his hands.

The next morning we took a short bus ride and went to a second-hand car yard, where Angus began looking the cars over. The car dealer came out and got talking. He and Angus obviously knew each other and they did a deal on a tidy-looking Humber Super-snipe with four hundred quid on it. Angus reckoned he could find a buyer for it, for a ten per cent commission. We got a change-of-ownership form off the dealer and drove away in the car. It was as simple as that. Angus had apparently done a bit of this before, and yet I found out later that he'd never had a driver's licence. I had to do the driving.

He directed me to another car yard, where, after half an hour of intense negotiation, Angus traded the Super-snipe in on a big Nash Rambler with six hundred quid on it. Angus beat him down to five hundred and sixty. As we drove away in the Nash Angus remarked that we'd just made at least seventy-five quid, but it wasn't the right sort of car for what he wanted, so we cruised past a few other car yards until we saw what Angus wanted and went in and did a clean swap of the Nash for a very nice one-owner, low-mileage Austin Cambridge. The dealer kept protesting that there was nothing in the deal for him but Angus talked him into it by subtly rubbishing the Austin and pointing out the superior qualities of the Nash, which was too flashy for his mother.

We arrived at the Commercial Travellers Club in the Austin at lunchtime. Angus bowled in as though we owned the place and ordered two beers and within a few minutes he was telling a bunch of blokes in suits this incredible yarn about how he had to sell his mother's car to cover medical expenses and those thieving car dealers would only offer him half what it was worth. They had him over a barrel, he was forced to sell the car but he wasn't going to let them get away with it on principle. He was going to sell it privately for what the dealers had offered him. Someone was going to get one hell of a bargain, but it wouldn't be those ratbag car dealers.

He was so convincing I wanted to buy the car off him myself, but I'd have had to be quick. A bloke who'd been listening just along the bar came up and asked Angus where the car was. They went outside to have a look at it and take it for a drive and when they returned half an hour later the car was sold. Seven hundred and fifty quid. The new owner drove us to a bank, where we cashed his cheque, the ownership papers were signed over and the deal was done.

We got a bus to the car dealer where we'd bought the Nash and told him we'd decided to pay cash and got him to tear up the Hire Purchase Agreement and gave him the five hundred and sixty quid. The dealer knew he'd been wroughted in some way but apart from being a bit surly there was nothing he could do about it. He had to accept the money.

From there we went back to the place where we got the Humber and paid the bloke for it, less forty quid commission. We'd made two hundred and thirty quid. Angus could have gone on doing that all day. I was impressed, but Angus played down his brilliant salesmanship. He reckoned it was just a matter of keeping an eye on what was worth what and where it was. He didn't like dealing with cars, it was too much like hard work to him. He preferred to do the small deals he found in the newspapers and a bit of discreet bidding at auctions. Much less hectic and less likely to bring on an attack of his spondylating leptospirosis.

There's no doubt that Angus could have been wealthy if he'd wanted to be. He pointed out many money-making opportunities in the papers that were too strenuous for him. If you quoted for this, or tendered for that, or bought up these or marketed those, or sat on them. . .

All these things needed was a bit of energy put on them, but that's what Angus didn't have, and only he could buy and sell things the way he bought and sold them. He chose only the simplest and least demanding bargains and managed to get by. Everyone who knew him agreed that Angus was a bit of a hypochondriac. Gifted, but too lazy to be bothered making anything of himself. His own worst enemy, was the general consensus of opinion.

Despite the outrageous messes he made, I grew quite fond of Angus. Our paths parted when my mate came back from overseas and I took to the road again, but I ran into Angus in Wellington a few months later, and again later still in Dunedin. He was always battling along doing small deals and getting kicked out of flats and rooms because of the terrible mess he made of them. He stayed with me for a month in Dunedin and got us kicked out of the flat for storing twelve naked mannequins in the front room until he could get a sale for them. You could see them through the curtains. It was a disturbing sight and there'd been a number of complaints.

I hadn't seen Angus for more than a year and when I was talking to a mutual friend I learned that Angus had died suddenly in Dunedin a few weeks before. It's always a bit sobering to hear that one of your mates has passed on, but it was doubly sobering when I was told that the official cause of death had been given as spondylating leptospirosis.

HAMMERHEAD

IN THE LATE sixties I was doing freelance interviews and skits for television, which was just getting off the ground here. They paid us fifteen dollars an item, which wasn't enough to live on, but I enjoyed doing it, so I bought a thirty-five-foot launch, the *Sunray,* and made a few bucks long-lining for snapper in the Hauraki Gulf. I'd do a few television items to keep them going and then I'd go fishing for a week or two.

It keeps you busy, running a long-line boat on your own, baiting the hooks, shooting the lines and picking them up and handling the boat at the same time, but I was getting a few baskets of fish on an average day and managing to keep my head above water. I sold my fish to a bloke who had a set-up in Whangaparapara Harbour on Great Barrier Island where I often anchored at night.

I was tied up in the Fisherman's Basin in Auckland one day, loading supplies for a trip out to the Barrier, when a bloke came along and asked me where I was going. When I told him Great Barrier Island he asked me if I could take him and three other adults and three children to Port Fitzroy, at the northern end of the island. They had the use of a house there for a month and the supply boat wasn't going out there for several days.

Fitzroy was fine with me. I told him I was leaving in about an hour and he hurried off to get his crew organised. They arrived in two taxis, two couples and three teenage kids and so much gear and tucker we had trouble finding space to stow it all.

We cast off and cruised up the channel and out into the

151

Gulf in perfect conditions. The women and youngsters were down in the cabin and the two blokes were in the wheelhouse with me. They were new to the area and asked me questions about the various islands and landmarks you could see. I didn't know a hell of a lot about them myself, but I let them get the impression that I was a weather-beaten old seafarer, and had been doing it for donkey's years.

There wasn't a breath of wind and the sea was smooth as glass. It was sweltering hot and we were soon stripped down to our shorts. We made good time and about four miles from the entrance to Fitzroy Harbour I cut the motor and let the *Sunray* drift to a stop and dived over the side to cool off. In no time everyone was into their togs and splashing in the sea all around the boat.

When I'd cooled off I climbed back on board and got ready to carry on, but everyone was having such a good time I didn't like to break it up. The kids were diving off the bow of the boat and shouting and splashing each other and the adults were diving off the stern and swimming around. Waiting for all of them to be on board at once was like trying to get drunks out of a pub.

I was keen to get going. If I could get them ashore at Fitzroy I might have just enough time to bait up and shoot a couple of long-lines before dark and take advantage of the good weather. I couldn't be bothered explaining all that to them so I told one of the men that it might be a good idea to get everyone on board because a big hammerhead shark usually goes through here at this time of day.

"A shark?" he said, looking around. "You'd better come aboard," he called out. "The skipper says there's a shark around!"

"A shark?" they all said, treading water.

That got them on board. And the last of the youngsters was still standing on the platform at the stern when a dirty big hammerhead shark came swimming up from astern of us with its dorsal fin out of the water. Eight or ten feet long, plenty big enough to give you a thrill. It had no doubt been attracted by all the activity in the water. I was as stunned as the rest of them. We watched as it swam up to within twenty feet of the boat and round it once and then disappeared down into the water. The bloke was staring at me.

"You cut that a bit fine, didn't you?" he said accusingly.

"Sorry about that," I said, starting the motor and lining her up on Fitzroy. "He's running a bit early today."

The poor bloke couldn't help staring at me. He was incredulous. He couldn't figure out how I'd been able to pick the exact spot, miles out in the open sea, and the exact time a shark was going to appear. I'd even nominated the exact type of shark it was going to be.

As a matter of fact I didn't know there were any hammerhead sharks in those waters. I'd certainly never seen one before, and I never saw another one there after that.

All the way to Fitzroy I could tell that bloke was wanting to say something, and when we were shaking hands on the wharf he suddenly blurted out, "You didn't *really* know that shark was going to be there did you?"

I casually lit my cigarette and blew a stream of smoke into the air. I couldn't let the poor bloke go running around for the rest of his life with a perplexity like that in his head.

"Relax, mate," I said. "I got a bigger bloody fright than you did."

A Piece of Hell

AT ONE PART of it I was living in the hamlet of Te Teko in the Bay of Plenty, guiding tourists on hunting, fishing and jet-boating trips. My partner and I had access through a bloke's farm to a block of fern and scrub and second-growth along the eastern side of Lake Matahina. The hunting there was good and you hardly ever failed to get a deer or a pig.

I was up there one day on my own and caught a nice eating-pig with my dogs. I dragged it out to the main track and lit a fire and singed the bristles off it. Before I left there I got a burning stick from the fire and poked it into a clump of dead fern beside the track in the hope of burning off a patch of ground for the deer to come out on in the spring. We'd done that in several places around there with good results. The fern wouldn't burn properly so I gave up on it and took my pig down the track to the ute and headed off home.

Stopping to open the gate at the back of the farm, I looked back up the hill and saw a goodly plume of smoke going up. My fire might have taken after all. Good. At the next gate there was no doubt about it. The plume of smoke had become a column. With a bit of luck we'd get a good burn-off.

By the time I got down to the road the column of smoke had become a skyscraper, and by the time I got home it was a rolling billowing wall. You could easily see it from our place seven miles away. A strong wind was getting up and I began to hope the fire hadn't jumped a creek that should have stopped it. Within an hour it was obvious that it had jumped the creek.

There was too much smoke going up for anything else to have happened. It was now into an expanse of scrub and fern that went for miles.

By that night the sky was orange with reflection from my fire and I was hoping it wouldn't jump the narrow gorge at the head of the lake and get into the thousands of acres of the Matahina Pine Forest. There's always a bit of extra paranoia about fire in a pine forest area. I was up and down all night looking anxiously for signs of the fire abating. The wind had dropped away but by this time the fire was creating its own wind and with no road access to the area ahead of it there was no way they could bulldoze a fire-break. There must have been a bit of panic going on up there, but no more panic than was going on in me. I didn't get much sleep that night.

By dawn the choppers were out, trying to douse the burning scrub nearest to the forestry with monsoon buckets. Extra fire appliances and truckloads of men from nearby Kawerau roared through Te Teko, heading for the threatened pines. The radio news informed us that the fire was raging out of control on a broad front and fire crews had been out patrolling all night. They suspected the fire had been deliberately lit by pig hunters. There were only two of us who had permission to use the access to that block and my partner was away on a fishing trip. They had to find out it was me, if they didn't know already.

My wife and I bundled the kids into the ute and we drove out to have a look at my handiwork. We went along the forestry side of the lake and stopped where we could get a good view of it. It was awesome. The fire was burning right along the edge of the lake and was two-thirds of the way to the top of the main ridge. It roared and leapt in fifty-foot flames, engulfing everything in its path. The heat was fantastic. You could feel it from where we were a quarter of a mile away. I saw a lone pine tree fifty or sixty yards from the advancing fire spontaneously burst into flames and set fire to the fern and scrub around it. The destructive power of a big bush fire is real scary to look at, especially when you realise you started it yourself with a little bit of burning stick. Burning whirling embers were being sucked hundreds of feet into the air by the intense heat it was generating.

Three helicopters, one from as far away as Rotorua, were clattering back and forth dunking their monsoon buckets in the lake and emptying them onto outbreaks of fire. A fixed-wing spotter plane circled overhead, fire appliances, trucks and utes raced urgently back and forth with their radios crackling, but all this technology and manpower was helpless to do anything about the piece of hell that was raging just across the river. They could only hope to stop it getting into the pines.

I decided to leave this to the experts. No point in torturing myself any more by gazing upon what I'd done. We drove over to Ruatahuna to visit some friends of ours, but all they could talk about was the big scrub fire over at Matahina. On our way home that night there was a most disturbing orange glow in the sky over Matahina. We could see it from Galatea, thirty miles away, so we carried on to Rotorua and stayed the night there.

The following day the radio and newspapers informed us that the fire had burned away from the forestry and was beginning to burn itself out. It was no longer considered a serious threat, but they were maintaining a vigilant watch on the remaining pockets of it. It had completely wiped out two thousand acres of scrub country. We went home and waited. If they made me pay for the cost of all that fire fighting I was more than ruined. A news item carried the information that the fire had cost an estimated quarter of a million dollars.

I lived in a state of constant apprehension for two days after that, and when the forestry boss pulled into our gateway on the third day I wanted to rush out and confess everything to him and beg him to punish me and get it over with. The forestry boss, Burt, was a good bloke. I knew him quite well, we did a bit of hunting together, but he wasn't here this time to jack up a hunting trip. He'd come to talk to me about that fire and we both knew it.

"G'day Crumpy."

"G'day Burt."

We sat on the steps in the sun and my wife made us a cup of tea. We talked about the weather, what the hunting had been like lately, when the plaster was coming off his daughter's wrist, who was going to win the test, how a dog he'd got off me was shaping up, the new couple who'd taken over the store, how his spuds were doing. . .

We talked about almost everything except fire. Finally Burt put his empty mug down and said he'd better get going. I walked to his ute with him and just as he was getting into it he stopped.

"By the way Crumpy," he said.

"What?" I croaked, knowing this was it.

"Leave your bloody matches at home next time you go up there will you?"

"I sure will," I promised.

Burt's face was inscrutable as he drove away. There was something he wasn't telling me. I'd seen Burt sack a man on the spot for taking too long to change a fanbelt. I was still uneasy, I'd got off too lightly. They didn't let people off scot-free who light fires in a forestry area, especially one the size of mine. I was waiting on a visit from the police at least, but for some reason they were keeping me in suspense.

Burt let me sweat on it for a couple of weeks before he put me out of my misery. It was up to the Logging Company, as owners of the land, to decide whether to prosecute me or not, and they'd decided not to. As it turned out I'd done them a favour. They'd been planning to clear that block for planting in pines but they hadn't even thought of using fire, it was far too

157

risky. They'd been going to put the scrub-crushers into it, a big and costly operation. Now the land was clear they could start planting it, months ahead of schedule and thousands of dollars inside their budget.

"But don't do it again, eh," warned Burt.

"Don't worry, Burt," I assured him. "I'm never going through that again if I can possibly help it."

THE EASTERN TOUCH

I WROTE A book once called *Bastards I Have Met* and the publishers shied off the title. So I published it myself and a few weeks later I had more money in my kick than I'd ever dreamed of, so I decided to have a look around the world and ended up with twenty-eight countries stamped in my passport.

I had many adventures. At one part of it I bought a BMW motorbike in Germany and set off to ride it to India, with the loose idea that I might ride it all the way back to New Zealand if I felt like it.

The first night out of Germany I camped in a camping ground in Austria, and in the night some slippery customer slit my little tent with a razor blade and cut open my leather coat and got my wallet out of the inside pocket and took all my money, leaving my passport and travellers cheques and papers on the ground outside the ruined tent. In the morning I had to go back to the border to get some more cash and then into Salzburg to buy a new tent and a coat.

That day I bowled a bloke in a town called Graz. It was his fault and he paid me exactly what it cost to fix the damage to my bike, but I was stuck in a camping ground there for three days while it was getting fixed.

I'd heard about stomach problems in these countries I was travelling through and I was interested to see how far I would get before it happened to me. It happened in Yugoslavia, or whatever they call it now, and caused some embarrassing adventures that I've just decided to keep to myself.

In Bulgaria I had a spectacular prang. Some women in blue smocks had dug a trench right across the road and they stood there drinking out of tins and watched me come blatting up the road and barrel into their trench and go somersaulting through the air and bounce and sprawl along the road.

The bike and I were both damaged but I got us going and carried on to Turkey, where my new coat and my best pair of goggles got swiped off the bike while I was getting my passport stamped at the border.

I spent a couple of days looking around Istanbul, and found out later that I had the Turkish money figured out all wrong and I'd been handing out staggering sums of money to the beggars in the streets. By the time I'd bought a new coat I was considerably over what I'd budgeted for this stage of the trip, but I'd been told things got cheaper the further east you went.

I couldn't figure out where the Turks kept all their women hidden, I hardly saw any, but the men sure lived up to their reputation. They were the wildest drivers I'd ever come across, and by the time I'd made it through Turkey I'd had a few hair-raising close shaves on the road and a number of minor prangs. The headlight, the front mudguard, both mirrors, the clutch-lever and one footrest had been broken off the bike, but it still went and I was still in one piece.

The Turkish/Iranian border wasn't a very elaborate set-up. My passport and papers were in order and I got through the border out of Turkey without any trouble, but when I went to go through the border into Iran I struck a snag in the form of a shady-looking customs officer. He carefully scrutinised my papers and stared at my saddle bags hanging over my shoulder. Finally he looked at me with pursed lips.

"You got drugs," he stated.

"No I haven't," I said. "I've got no drugs."

"You got drugs," he repeated.

160

He was speaking very quietly and menacingly and I thought of something not very nice that I'd recently heard happened to a European couple who'd been thrown into an Iranian jail for something they didn't do.

"No drugs," I said. "Search me, search my bags."

He leaned over the counter towards me. I could smell the garlic on his breath.

"I say you got drugs, you got drugs," he murmured, "and I say you not got drugs, you not got drugs."

"Well I not got drugs," I said.

He shook his head. "No," he said, flicking his bloodshot eyes towards the duty-free shop between the two borders. "You only not got drugs when you go over there and get me a bottle of whisky."

I looked across at the duty free shop and then back at him.

"Who's going to pay for it?" I said.

"You are," he grinned.

"Cut it out," I said. "I don't mind getting it for you, but you'll have to pay for it yourself."

"Then you got drugs," he sighed, spreading his palms regretfully.

"Okay," I said, "I not got drugs."

I crossed the road and bought him a bottle and got them to wrap it up and brought it back and put it on the counter in front of him. He put it out of sight under the counter.

"No drugs," I said.

"No drugs," he agreed seriously.

He stamped my passport and folded my papers and handed them to me.

"Welcome to our country, sir," he said. "I hope you enjoy your stay."

I scampered out of there and took off into Iran. I wanted to be well away from there when that customs officer had a look at what I'd got him from the duty-free shop. It was a bottle of the cheapest local plonk they sold.

They got me, though, in ancient Persia. By the time I got to Teheran my bike was playing up and I had to leave it with the agents and wait several days for parts. That put me on the hoof and left me vulnerable to those wily Persians.

The city was teeming with people, all trying to flog something, even if it was only a hard luck yarn. A pretty young girl with big brown serious eyes and a neatly ironed school uniform bailed me up and told me how their school had been burnt down by bad men and they were taking up a collection for a new school. She showed me a grubby clipboard with the names of donors on it and how much they'd given. Most of the donations were ten rials and the smallest I had was a twenty-rial note so I asked if she had any change and she said she didn't have any. I was her first customer of the day and she'd given all her previous donations to the Headmistress the night before. I shrugged and handed her the twenty-rial note and as soon as I held the money out to her she underwent a sudden transmogrification, from a pathetic waif to a predatory Persian tigress, snatched the money and ran off into the jungle and was quickly swallowed up in the seething undergrowth. She'd only have to do that a few times a day to make more money than her old man probably did.

Determining not to let myself get ripped off like that again, I went into an eating house and had a feed of curried mutton and rice and when I went to pay for it I was informed that the price wasn't ten rials, as it said on their blackboard, that was yesterday's price. Today's price was twenty rials. I paid up.

I found a small room and rented it for twenty rials a night and I'd no sooner dumped my saddlebags on the couch when a veiled woman appeared at the door and begged me in passable English to let her do my washing for me. Twenty rials. I had a bit of dirty washing, a pair of jeans, a singlet, a T-shirt and a shirt, so I dug them out and gave them to her and told her I'd pay her when she brought them back.

I never saw her again. I found out later that my Levi's jeans were worth a small fortune around there. I complained to my landlord about it.

"What did she look like, saab?" he said.

"Like her," I said, pointing to a woman walking past completely veiled and enveloped in black robes.

"I'm sorry, saab," said the landlord, "but if you go and give your clothes to strange women. . . " he shrugged.

I was having a look around the city and was accosted on a corner in a bazaar by a well-dressed young man who politely enquired if I'd like to buy some excellent carpet at very reasonable rates. I explained to him that I was travelling on a motor bike. That was no trouble, he assured me. All I had to do was leave my address with him and he'd personally see that it was consigned to any address in the world I wanted.

"No bloody carpet," I said firmly.

"Gold," he said. "I can get you gold at world-lowest prices."

"No gold."

"Turquoise? Best turquoise in Iran!"

"No turquoise either, thanks mate."

"You want a girl?" he said. "I got beautiful girls!"

"No girls."

"Hashish? I got best Afghani hashish!"

"No, mate. No hashish either."

I finally got rid of him. They can be pretty persistent some of those Persians.

The parts for my bike still hadn't arrived and I decided to have a look around one of the mosques to pass the time. I was directed to a big domed building with pillars and inlaid marble floors. There was a row of shoes lined up along the wall at the entrance so I took my boots off and put them there and went inside.

There were about thirty Persian blokes kneeling on carpets, devotedly praying to Allah. I felt a bit embarrassed, only being in there for a look, so I mumbled the Lord's Prayer, had a look round and left. I wouldn't have been in there more than fifteen minutes, but when I went to get my boots they were gone. My irreplaceable American cavalry boots that I'd got off an army officer and turned down big offers for. It was hard to believe that such deeply religious people would swipe something out of one of their own churches. I arrived back at my little room in a pair of plastic sandals, for which I'd paid twenty rials.

The next day I found a pair of buffalo-hide, hand-stitched boots in the bazaar. They looked okay but they were uncomfortable and they leaked. There was some good news that day. My bike was fixed, I could leave this place, but they had one last snip at me before I left. The repairs to my bike cost fifteen thousand rials, probably more than the bike was worth. That rocked me. It was no use arguing with them. They had an itemised bill made out and I didn't know what anything was worth around there. I had to pay it. It was now a matter of how far I was going to get before I ran out of money.

The further east I got the harder-up everyone was. I was determined not to give any more money to beggars, I just couldn't afford it, but in Harat in Afghanistan I gave a crying woman some money to buy medicine for her crying baby. She assured me that the baby was going to die without it. Later that day I saw her sitting on a bench on a muddy back-street corner with two other women, drinking wine from bottles in paper bags and shouting abuse at some women across the street.

The Afghanis must have thought I looked vulnerable because they tried to sell me guns of all descriptions – including hand-made muzzle-loaders and pistols – and knives, daggers, and swords. I bought an embroidered handkerchief.

Over the Khyber Pass to Peshawar in Pakistan. I was coming off the bike on an average of once a day. The bike was badly knocked around but still going, but it wasn't charging and I had to pay a bloke in Rawalpindi to fix the alternator for me. He ripped me off handsomely but I had to pay him.

By this time I didn't have enough money left for my fare back to New Zealand and I still had a fair way to go before I could get to an airport. I just had to keep going and see what happened, and plenty did.

In Lahore I ran into a sacred cow that walked right out in front of me. I careered off it and crashed into a crowded eating house. I had to pay for damage to the eating house and wheeled the bike away down the street pursued by a crowd of outraged cow-worshippers.

By the time I made it to Amritsa in India my bike was a wreck. The forks were bent and rigid, no headlight, clutch lever or front brake, the tank was dented (from a thrown brick), the handlebars were twisted awry and the frame was buckled, but it was still going. My saddlebags were worn through in several places from being scraped along the road. But I'd made it to India.

At a camping ground in Lahore I met an Australian couple who warned me to be super-careful of the Indians ripping me off. They'd bought a brand new Volkswagon pop-top caravan in Europe and were driving it home to Australia. They'd made the mistake of camping in the open in a grove of trees outside New Delhi and woke up in the morning looking at the sky. The Indians had cut the pop-top out of it. The van was up on blocks and all the wheels were gone. The windscreen was gone and their radio and a lot of their personal possessions had been stolen, including all their money. They were ruined. By the time they'd sold what was left of their van they had just enough money to make it back to Europe. They didn't even know how they were going to eat. I didn't know how I was going to eat either, but I had to give them a hundred dollars to help them out.

I felt sorry for that couple but I couldn't see anything like that happening to me. I always camped in camping grounds and slept with my tent tied onto my bike and my saddlebags under my head and my money and papers in a leather pouch tucked down the front of my jeans. But I was no match for Indian ingenuity. The next day in New Delhi they got me the best yet.

I figured I had about five hundred rupees' worth of travellers cheques left and decided to change them all into rupees and maybe cable a mate of mine in New Zealand for money or something. We'd been told at the border that the authorities would take no responsibility for anyone changing money on the street. They offer you a better exchange rate, but I wasn't taking any risks with my last few dollars.

I found a branch of the Bank of India in a narrow street and went in. There was a smooth-looking Indian bloke in a suit behind the counter. I told him I'd like to change some travellers cheques into rupees.

No trouble, sir, he told me. The exchange rate was particularly favourable just then. He passed me a pen and I signed the cheques and pushed them across to him and gave him his pen back. He put the pen in his pocket, picked up the cheques, said one moment sir, and went through a door behind him.

I looked around the room and it slowly dawned on me that there was nothing in there. No calendars on the walls, no paper anywhere, the place was bare. I ran round the end of the counter and opened the door the bloke had just gone through with the last of my money. There was an empty office there, and another door that opened out onto a teeming Indian street.

I went back out the front door and stood looking up at the peeling sign across the front of the building that said BANK OF INDIA. It had no doubt been a genuine branch of the Bank of India in the past.

Well, this was it. I'd set off with enough money to get me right around the world, and here I was in New Delhi with less than twenty rupees in my pocket and a beaten-up motor bike entered on my passport that I couldn't leave India without surrendering unconditionally to the Indian government. They'd beaten me, I was a babe in the woods amongst this lot.

I found the New Zealand Embassy and asked to be repatriated. The people at the Embassy got a message to my mate in New Zealand to send me some money and an air ticket and they arrived the next day by magic of satellite. Five days later I was back in the bush on the West Coast wondering how all that had happened.

A man's an easy touch, I guess, but in a way I reckon I got good value for my money out of the Eastern touch. Wouldn't have missed it for quids.

THE LAST BRUMBY

*I wrote this story in memory of the thousands of beautiful wild
horses that roamed the central North Island tussock country in
the 1950s. They've nearly all been shot.*

T**HE OLD MAN** lived alone in a two-roomed shack near
the bush edge, two hundred yards from the river. It was
an old post-splitters' hut, built there when you could get
five pounds a hundred for split red-beech posts. No electricity,
just a wood stove and a kerosene lamp. A two-hundred-gallon
tank outside collected rain-water off the roof. He cut his firewood
with a bow-saw and split it on the woodblock at one
end of the hut.

He used a little corrugated-iron shed behind the hut for
storing a bit of gear and hanging his possum skins in. There
was a three-acre holding paddock in front of the hut that he
kept his horse in, and a set of stockyards made from split rails
that were built when they ran cattle up the river flats. The grazing
lease had expired years before and reverted to the Crown and
they'd never allowed it to be renewed.

There was a track into the place from the main road, two
miles downriver, but no metalled road. The old man didn't mind
that, he didn't drive a vehicle. He rode out to the pub on the
highway once a month to collect his pension and order his
supplies for the next month. It didn't cost him much to live.

He'd moved out here seven years before, after his wife
died. He had some kids, two girls and a boy. He hadn't seen any

168

of them for years now and when asked about them he could only say that they were "runnin' around somewhere". He could remember what they were like when they were at school but now he didn't know if he would have recognised them.

His only company these days was his horse and a black-and-tan dog called Dog. He kept it chained to a fencing standard banged into the ground beside a 44-gallon drum out on one side of the hut when he wasn't going anywhere. Half a dozen bantam chooks and a rooster made up the rest of his family. It was a lonely life but he'd got used to it.

He stood in the doorway of the hut with a mug of tea cupped in his hands. It was overcast. Might rain later. He finished his tea, put the mug on the bench beside his washing-up basin, put on his boots and hat and went out and got an armful of dry wood and some split kindling and put it in the woodbox beside the stove. Then he got his saddle and bridle from the shed and took them over to the horse paddock.

The mare was a bit hard to catch at times and the old man wasn't in any shape to chase horses around paddocks these days, so he had eighty feet of braided nylon rope trailing behind her. She trotted into a corner of the paddock and he followed over and picked up the end of the rope. Once she was caught she was easy enough to handle. She was a short stocky horse, which was a good way to have them when you've got a bit of arthritis in one of your hips. He'd caught her up the valley with a noose set under a ducking-stick on a horse track through some scrub and taken his time breaking her in.

He put the bridle on her and led her across to the saddle, hung the reins over a post, put the saddle-sack on her and swung the saddle onto her back and girthed it up. Then he coiled up the rope and tied it to the saddle with a bootlace without untying the end from round the horse's neck. He went back to the hut for his oilskin coat and the split sack he tied behind the saddle to carry stuff in, let the dog off, and he was ready. He opened the gate and awkwardly mounted the horse and rode away up the valley at a brisk walk.

The only sounds were the plodding of the horse's hooves, with the regular click of a loose front shoe, as he made his way along the track that wound through the tussock, with the dog trotting along a few yards in front. High above him two red deer bounced up a ridge, paused for a few moments looking down at him and then disappeared into the bush. He had some venison hanging up at the hut and hadn't bothered bringing his rifle.

An hour's ride up the valley he turned off to a cut track that zigzagged its way up through bush for several hundred feet and then came out on an open plateau a mile across and three miles long. It had been a lake up until a few hundred years before, when an earthquake had split the ground at one end of it and drained it. Now it was a big tussock plain surrounded by native bush and scrub, with several swampy areas of flax and toi-toi and cabbage trees and manuka and raupo. These swamps were home to pukeko, several species of wild duck and quite a bit of other bird life – pheasant, quail, tui, weka, banded rail and blue heron. The old man often got a feed from there, mostly duck. The bushline around the edge of the plain was good deer-stalking and his dog sometimes caught a pig there for his camp oven.

He rode up a tussock gully that had once been an arm of the lake to check six possum traps he'd set the day before. He made a bit of extra money running trap lines around the edge of the bush, and it gave him something to do. He wanted to find out if the skins were coming right. He'd caught four possums but the furs weren't ready yet so he left the traps sprung and hung the possums in a tree for dog tucker. Then he rode further round the bushline.

After about half an hour he rounded a bend and saw a mob of wild horses out on the tussock. There were three mobs of them up here, each with a leading stallion that kept them within strict territorial boundaries. There was a yarn that a truckload of horses had gone over the bank out on the highway and released some thoroughbred brood mares among the brumbies.

There were many theories about how the wild horses had got there. When he was a young bloke there'd been wild horses all through the region, but now these were the only ones left. It was a great sight to see a mob of brumbies sweeping and thundering across the plain, with the stallion always running at the rear of his mob.

This particular mob belonged to a stallion the old man liked the look of. He was magnificent. Beautiful. Almost black with white fetlocks, mane and tail. Looked as though he could have a bit of Arab in him. As soon as the old man rode into sight the stallion paraded between him and his mares, neck and tail arched, hardly touching the ground, snorting, wheeling and prancing back and forth, while his mares cantered away to the bush and disappeared up horse tracks in the scrub. The stallion stood on a rise prancing and alert to make sure they weren't followed. The old man sat on his horse and watched him for a while. Then he gave the stallion a friendly wave and turned and rode back the way he'd come.

The stallion was used to the old man riding around on his territory but they always had to go through this ritual. It was a kind of formality they had going between them and the stallion never let him get any closer than this.

He rode back across the plain, picking up his possums on the way, and down to the valley and back to the hut. He'd been away for about five hours. He put the mare in the paddock, skinned a possum for the dog and tied him up, washed his hands and face at the tank-stand and lit the stove. By the time he'd peeled a few spuds for his evening meal the tea billy was boiling. He made a brew, turned on his transistor radio – always on the National Programme – and settled down in his sacking chair with the door of the firebox open to let a bit of warmth out into the hut.

A fairly typical day, but it wasn't over yet. He was dozing off in his chair when the dog started barking. Something was coming. The old man got up and went to the door. A Department of Conservation four-wheel-drive ute was bouncing across the tussock towards the hut. The old man got along okay with the DOC blokes. He didn't agree with some of their policies but that wasn't the fault of the blokes in the field. They'd left him pretty much alone, which was all he wanted.

The ute pulled up at the hut and two blokes got out. One of the head rangers, a bloke called Taggart, and one of his rookies. They'd brought him a loaf of fresh bread, a cabbage and a newspaper. They'd also brought some news that was going to affect the old man's lifestyle.

All the land around here that wasn't in native bush was going to be planted in radiata pine as part of a government work-scheme, including the big flat. They wouldn't want anyone living here because of the fire risk. He was going to have to move out within a year. The hut would probably be pulled down.

The old man shrugged. He'd moved on before, and he knew of other huts he could use. There was one on a station where he'd worked on and off for years and they'd invited him to use it and lend a hand with a bit of stock work. That's probably what he'd end up doing.

The DOC blokes respected his knowledge of the area and sometimes asked him about opossum and deer and pig concentrations. This time they wanted to know how many wild horses he reckoned were living up on the big flat. He told them, a hundred and thirty-odd. They explained that they were going

172

to have to get rid of them before they could start planting because of the damage horses do to pine seedlings. They trample them, or nip the tops out of them, either lifting them out of the ground or distorting the shape of the trees. They would have to be destroyed. The old man knew the horses wouldn't stand a chance once they started heading them off and shooting them from their helicopters. They'd simply get them milling around out in the open and pick them off. There was nothing he or the horses could do about it.

When the DOC blokes had gone the old man stoked up the stove and put his billy of spuds on and sat down with a fresh mug of tea and had a bit of a think. By the time he climbed into his bunk that night he'd decided to have a go at trying to save that stallion.

The next morning he was up early. He cleaned the ashes out of the stove and lit the fire, had a brew of tea and heated and ate a can of beef casserole with toast and fresh eggs, cleaned up his billies and dishes, swept the hut and then got out his old .303 Lee Enfield army rifle. He dragged the pull-through through it a few times and then squinted at the sky through the shiny rifled barrel. Then he put the bolt and magazine in it, grabbed a handful of ammunition and went down to the river, where he propped himself up on a ridge of earth and carefully sighted it in on a white stone you could circle with your finger and thumb, fifty yards away in a bank across the river, and squeezed off a shot.

His second shot shattered the stone out of the bank and after a few more shots at different targets at different distances he was satisfied that the rifle and he were shooting as accurately as they were going to. He went back and caught the mare and clinched the loose shoe tight and saddled up, tied an extra length of rope on the saddle, let the dog off and rode up the valley with the rifle slung across his shoulders.

Up on the big flat he rode across to the bush edge and along it for a while, then up a scrubby gut on a horse track and into the bush, where he tied the mare to a tawa tree. He coiled the long rope round his chest and shoulder and fed three bullets into the magazine of the rifle. He knew he wasn't even going to get that many chances. Then he set off walking through the bush, keeping the dog in behind him.

He had a fair idea where the stallion and his mares would be, and he turned out to be right. After half an hour he sneaked out to the bush edge and saw them out on the plain a bit further along. He cut back into the bush and circled round there, glad it was no further than this because his hip was starting to give him trouble.

He came out of the bush onto a low manuka spur and crawled through the scrub until he was in position as close to the stallion as he was going to get, about sixty-five yards from him. He was feeding a little apart from his mob, throwing up his head every few moments to check out the plain for intruders.

The old man rested the rifle in the forks of a manuka bush and carefully sighted on the stallion's neck. He waited until the horse had raised its head to look around, adjusted his aim, and squeezed off his shot. The stallion went down as though an anvil had fallen on him and the mares thundered away and gathered in a confused group and then poured into the bush just below where the old man was hobbling down the ridge as fast as he could go.

The horse was lying still as death. He didn't wait to check whether he'd killed it or not. He looped his rope around the back legs in several half-hitches and then did the same with the front legs and tied all four legs close together. Then he could relax and have a look at the animal. It was still breathing. He'd creased it high in the neck at the base of the mane, just behind the ears. His bullet had gone cleanly through and there wasn't

174

much blood. It looked like both he and the horse had been lucky. Looking at its teeth he estimated that it was about four years old, young for a stallion to have his own mares.

He was urinating on the wound to sterilise it when the stallion suddenly started coming round and the old man got back out of the way as the horse started struggling and snorting. All it could do was thrash its head around and struggle against the rope round its legs. He watched it for about twenty minutes until its struggles began to weaken. Then he left it there and limped back to where he'd left the mare and rode back to the hut, working out what he was going to do next.

The next morning he saddled up the mare and put on her the collar he used to snig his firewood down from the bush. Then he collected all the rope he could find and rode back up to the hog-tied stallion and tied the mare to a nearby tree. The mob of mares with their colts and fillies were milling around in confusion a few hundred yards away and soon disappeared around the bush edge. They would soon be absorbed into the other two mobs.

It had rained in the night and the stallion had churned up a patch of mud. His mouth and one of his eyes were full of dirt. As soon as the old man came near it started thrashing around again but it was getting a bit weak by this time and after a few minutes it lay still, staring up at him with rolled-back eyes. He stood near it for about fifteen minutes, letting it get used to his presence and his smell.

Within an hour he could stroke its nose and neck without it panicking. He got another rope knotted round its neck and brought the mare over and hitched the stallion onto the collar and dragged it by the neck across to a ribbonwood tree that grew on its own out from the bush and tied the horse to it, with about eight feet of slack in the rope. Then he had to leave it for about an hour to settle down again. When the stallion was lying quiet when he touched it he carefully undid the knot and unlooped the rope from around its legs and got quickly back out of the way.

As soon as the stallion found it could move its legs it staggered to its feet, nearly falling over, and tried to pull itself free, sitting back on its haunches and shaking its head from side to side and rearing and squealing. It was getting weak and after a few minutes of that it had to give in to the rope. It ended up standing there with its head down, hollow-flanked and covered with mud. It tried to pull back again when the old man came near but when it felt the rope it gave in and just stood there, nervous but beaten. The old man reached out and touched the muscle-ridged, muddy neck, ready to duck behind the tree if the horse got nasty. It twitched at his touch and then just stood there.

The old man spent the rest of the day coming and going, getting the horse used to the process and by late afternoon he decided he wasn't going to make any more progress with the stallion that day. He rode off home leaving it tied to the tree.

The next morning he took a plastic bucket up there and carried water from a swamp a few hundred yards out on the plain. The stallion performed a bit when he came near it but within half an hour it was slurping greedily at a second bucket of water. The old man continued gentling him and by that night he could lead the stallion around on a short rope, though he still had it tied to the tree on a long rope. It was leading quite well, following him around with the rope slack. It wasn't vicious, as he feared it might be. He tied it short to the tree, gave it another pat and got another bucket of water for it and went home.

He handled the stallion again all the next day, getting it accustomed to being mucked around with. It was becoming obedient, but still nervous. That evening he replaced several broken rails on the old stockyards.

The day after that the old man got the stallion settled down and then tied it to the mare's saddle and led him around the plain on a shorter rope. Round and round then down through the bush to the valley, where he let it have a feed from a grassy bank at the edge of the river. Then he walked him steady down the valley and got him into the stockyard and tied to a post with little trouble. He had him home.

Over the next week the old man spent most of the time with the stallion. He could lead him anywhere now, especially when they were going over to the river for a feed of the lush grass that grew along its banks. By this time he had a halter on him and it was easy to get a bit into his mouth and begin to mouth him, nice and gentle.

The stallion stiffened when the old man put a surcingle round him, and hunched when he carefully tightened it up, bit by bit, but by the end of the day he could put it on and take it off whenever he wanted. The stallion was beginning to learn how to learn, and beginning to like the old man, who he now associated with food and water. He even started getting in the habit of rubbing his head on the old man, which nearly knocked him over with his crook hip, but the old man had to put up with that.

His next move was to tie the stallion to a post in the yard, blindfold him and put the saddle, minus the stirrups, on his back and cinch it up. Then he tied a lot of stuff onto the saddle. A sack, an old red shirt, an aluminium pot, a holed gumboot, a couple of plastic containers — anything he could find around the place that would flap or rattle without coming off. Then he tied a blue plastic bag to the side of its halter. The stallion was trembling so hard he could hear it. Then he untied the rope off the halter and whipped the blindfold off and got up on the rail of the yard.

The stallion stood for a moment, then it shook its head

177

away from the plastic bag and then suddenly burst into a frenzied bucking and snorting and rearing and cow-kicking at its load. Round and round it went, almost going down when it crashed into the rails in a corner, until finally it was exhausted. It stood, white with sweat and heaving, the air whistling in its nostrils.

The old man left it there and went over to the hut and cut some firewood and turned on his radio and made a fresh brew of tea and ate some eggs and toast. Several times during the day he heard the stallion getting stuck into it again, but each time the thumping and rattling lasted for less time.

The next morning when the old man went over to the yard with a bucket of water the stallion threw a small tantrum but by now it knew it couldn't get rid of its load that way and soon gave up. The old man put the bucket of water through the rails and went back to the hut for breakfast. Looking back he saw that the stallion was drinking.

The next day the old man took the rifle across to the yard and fired a shot near the stallion. It started but stood there. He fired several more shots until the horse didn't even flinch at the blast. That afternoon he got into the yard with the stallion and it came up to him. He took the shredded plastic bag off the halter and tied the horse to a post and carefully, bit by bit, he removed its load. Then he rubbed it down with a sack and led it down to the river for a feed of grass.

That was the day he let the stallion out into the horse paddock with the mare. He'd done as much as he could to make the fence horse-proof, but the stallion didn't even try to get out over it. He fed around beside the mare as though he'd been doing it all his life.

By the end of another week the stallion was becoming a bit of a pet. A big powerful dangerous pet. He was easier to catch than the mare and every day the old man tied him up and put the saddle on him and led him around and then took it off again, sometimes two or three times.

It was time to ride him. As a younger man the old man would have been on him long before this, but with his crook hip and brittle bones he hadn't been game to risk it any sooner. He couldn't afford to get injured. He got the stallion in the yard and tied him to a post and saddled him up, led him to the middle of the yard, took a bit of tension on the reins and put one foot in the stirrup and put weight on it. The horse flinched away from the unaccustomed weight and then stood.

This was it. The old man swung himself into the saddle and groped with his foot for the other stirrup. The stallion snorted and side-stepped. The old man held him in with the reins and stood him there, letting him get used to the weight on his back, stroking his neck and talking quietly to him. Then he released the tension on the reins and gently urged the stallion forward and walked him round and round the yard, first one way then the other. He was responding nicely to the slightest pressure on the reins. The gentle mouthing was paying off.

After that the old man rode the stallion every day, first in the yard and then in the horse paddock and then down to the river, where he would let him feed around, moving further away from the hut every day. One day he took his rod and tied the horse to a washed-up log and caught a nice rainbow trout with a huhu grub in a big pool on a bend of the river.

Then one day when they were trotting along a flat at the edge of the river a cock pheasant suddenly flew out from right under the stallion's front feet. The stallion gave a start and leapt sideways and the old man came off. In the second before he crashed onto the ground and knocked himself out on a rock the old man had a vision of the stallion bolting away up the valley with his saddle.

As he came round the first thing he noticed was a rhythmical tearing sound. It was the stallion cropping grass a

179

few feet from his head. He climbed slowly to his feet and took the reins, retrieved his hat and put it on, led the horse over to a bank and got on him and rode back to the hut. He was sore and sprained and there was a big throbbing lump coming up on the side of his head, but what he could feel most was a sense of satisfaction.

The old man spent most of the next day in his bunk, resting his sprains and bruises, and within a few days he was back on his stallion, walking, trotting, cantering and galloping as the terrain allowed. The stallion was the most sure-footed horse he could remember riding. He could take him just about anywhere and do just about anything with him. It was a good feeling to have all that energy at his disposal. It had taken him a month.

It took the old man all one morning to get a set of shoes on the stallion. He wasn't going to be too hard to keep shod, once he got used to it. In the afternoon he rode out to the pub on the main road and arrived back at the hut in the dark with his supplies. The stallion had baulked a bit at the sight of his first motor vehicle, a stock truck that roared past him, but after a while he only pricked his ears at them.

A few mornings after that the old man was riding back down the valley with a deer he'd shot draped across the front of his saddle when two helicopters clattered across overhead. He turned the horse and watched them fly up the valley and lift up and across to the big flat. As he rode on he began to hear the popping of distant rifle shots. He reached forward and patted the stallion's powerful arched neck, pleased that he'd been able to save him from the slaughter that was going on up there.

Pleased and satisfied. He'd done what he'd set out to do. It hadn't been easy for a bloke as old and decrepit as him, but he'd done it. He'd caught and broken in the stallion he used to admire running free on the tussock plain with his mares, and now he had the last surviving brumby, and better legs under him than his own had ever been.

180

KURI

H E WAS A fairly big hunk of a dog, a three-year-old black and tan huntaway called Kuri. He belonged to a high-country shepherd called Pete, along with four other working dogs.

Nothing distinguished Kuri from any of the other dogs until his instincts overrode his training one day and he bit into a running merino ewe and tasted the hot thrilling flow of blood and involuntarily killed the sheep.

Kuri knew he'd done something wrong but he didn't know how wrong until the bullets were zinging off the rocks around him. He took refuge in a scrubby gully and followed it out onto a stud farm, where he killed three breeding ewes in the night, ate most of a hind-quarter and then moved further along the range at a lope that covered miles in minutes. By daylight he was twenty miles away on a station he'd mustered on the previous summer.

His strategy for survival evolved. His instincts told him not to stay around where he'd made a kill, especially after daylight when the men were about, so Kuri killed in the evenings and ate and then travelled many miles and slept through most of the days. In the evening he'd watch a homestead from a high ridge until the men were in from the hill, then he'd kill and eat and travel on.

Within three months Kuri had killed more than two hundred sheep along a forty-mile stretch of the mountains. He had his beat worked out. They knew it was him, every sheep-worrying dog has its own method of killing, its trade mark, and although Kuri was seen a number of times he always got away because people working on farms don't normally carry guns around with them.

Kuri became thoroughly wild. There were only three things in his life now, killing, eating and avoiding men. Killing was easy. He could kill thirty sheep in a night and be holed up miles away on another property by dawn. Eating was never a problem.

He'd tried other meat. Goat was all right but harder to catch than sheep, and they didn't have that exciting smell and taste. Rabbit was too quick and not much to eat. Possum was something of a treat but it was tricky to get. Possums could fight. Kuri had several scars on his nose from an encounter with a big buck possum on a moonlit track. Chasing the chamois high in the rocks and the deer in the bush was a waste of energy.

Nothing matched the primitive thrill and the taste and the accessibility of mutton. He could stalk up on a sheep grazing in the tussock and have it by the throat before it could move two body lengths.

A year went by and Kuri continued to dodge the bullet. It was being said that he'd killed so many sheep that if it had all been on one property it would have ruined them. One estimate put the figure at around thirteen hundred. The run-holders got together and posted a reward of five hundred dollars for Kuri's scalp. They also arranged to call up the deer-recovery helicopter when Kuri was sighted and try to get him that way.

Kuri didn't know any of this, he didn't know that the three men he'd been watching on the ridge across the valley had spotted him and called up the chopper on a cellphone. It came suddenly up over the ridge and was on him by the time he'd got running. Bullets were chopping into the ground around him. He felt something pluck at his side as an AK47 bullet creased him across the ribs.

He was running in a mad panic and it was lucky for him that he was running towards a block of beech bush. Suddenly he was in the trees and the chopper had had to bank away.

Three nights later Kuri killed seventeen in-lamb ewes on a station thirty miles further along the range. Someone suggested that it was revenge but it wasn't. Kuri didn't hate people, he was just afraid of them.

Another time Kuri was trotting along a bulldozed track when two hunters he hadn't scented or seen opened up on him with rifles. A .308 bullet hit him in the foot at more than 3,000 ft per second as he jumped off the track into some scrub. The hunters came running down after him but even on three legs they were easy for Kuri to evade. He followed the gully for a few hundred feet down the mountainside and was around the edge of a ridge and away into another gully while the hunters were still throwing rocks into the patch of scrub he'd first jumped into.

Kuri was inactive for a while after that and people were beginning to believe he was dead. Then they found twenty-seven dead lambs in a paddock with Kuri's trade mark all over them.

He wasn't sighted very often but when he was seen it was noticed that he now ran with a limp and his tracks indicated that he had a distorted left front foot. He was still more than a match for any sheep, though, and the slaughter continued. He was also more than a match for his pursuers. They had the chopper out after him several times but he always managed to evade them. Whenever Kuri was out and about in the daytime he was never far from cover. He'd learned that one.

On one property they put poison baits out for Kuri, and poisoned three of their own dogs. Kuri preferred his meat fresh and not smelling of men. On another occasion nineteen men encircled an area Kuri had been seen in to try to cut him off, but he was miles away by the time they'd got themselves organised.

He could be seen in one place and within an hour he could be seen somewhere else fifteen miles away.

My wife and I were living in an outback hut on a high-country run that was on Kuri's beat. We'd seen him a few times but never got a shot at him. He was real good at disappearing. The runholder had lost hundreds of sheep to Kuri and after three years they were no closer to nailing his hide on the wall than ever, further from it if anything. They were beginning to feel that it was hopeless. The dog had them outwitted, he was too cunning for them.

One day it was raining and my wife and I were spending the day in the hut. I went outside to get some firewood and saw Kuri standing up the hill. He turned and slouched limping around the hillside into the matagouri.

Our bitch was in season at the time and we had her shut in the shed because we didn't want her getting in pup. In case Kuri was hanging around after the bitch we set five possum traps around the back and side of the shed and stapled them to the walls and covered them with leaves and left the bitch chained up in the shed with the door open.

Nothing happened. We let the bitch out for a run in the daytime and tied her back in the shed at night. Again nothing happened. We decided that if nothing happened again we'd spring the traps and give up on it. Those traps were borrowed off our possum line and we needed them.

We were sound asleep when all hell broke loose out at the shed. Yowling and snarling and thrashing about. The dog, we've got him. We lit a candle and I grabbed the pump-action .22 and fed a handful of rounds into the magazine. My wife brought the candle and we went out to the shed. It was just beginning to break daylight. When Kuri saw us coming his snarling and yelping and struggling grew more desperate. He started biting at the leg that was caught in the trap and then as we came

184

closer he leapt at us, a big dark snarling shape in the candle-light, snatched back in mid-leap by the chain on the trap.

I started nervously pumping shots at him from the hip. My third bullet winged him and my fourth killed him. Suddenly he lay dead in the candle light. Sudden silence. It was over.

We went back into the hut and lit the fire and had a shaky cup of tea. When it was daylight we went out to have a look at Kuri. He lay there with his tongue hanging out the side of his mouth, big and rangy and scarred and club-footed. We were horrified to discover that he'd only been caught by one back toe. One more leap like the one he'd made at us would have pulled him free. But his number was up. Kuri was dead. Brought undone by that most irresistible of impulses, the mating instinct.

Looking at him lying there I wondered that something so harmless-looking could have caused so many people so much trouble and expense and done such a terrific amount of damage. Thousands of sheep killed, thousands of man-hours wasted, thousands of dollars lost and thousands of dollars spent, all over an ordinary-looking dog that lost control of its instincts one day.

We buried Kuri beside the creek and advised the run-holders that they'd never see him again. We didn't claim the five hundred dollar reward, we didn't want it. There's nothing very heroic or meritorious about shooting a dog in a trap. It was something that had to be done for the general good, though we'd have preferred not to have been the ones who had to do it.

THE BRAHMAN BULL

MY WIFE AND I were mining gold out the back of a high-country sheep and cattle station in Otago, living in an old miners' hut, perched hundreds of feet above the river to get a bit of winter sun. We were getting enough gold not to have to work too hard or too long to earn enough to live on. We'd do three or four hours' mining in the morning and after lunch we'd wash up our gold and maybe saddle the horses and ride around the countryside, or do a bit of gardening, or gather and cut some firewood, read a book or just sit in the sun. It was a good life.

In the evenings I liked to take a walk along a track that went around the mountainside from our hut. I enjoyed the atmosphere of those still, clear, tussocky Otago valleys, especially in the dusk. You could hear a small bird cheep across the other side of the valley.

It was wonderfully peaceful, right up until they stuck a big Brahman bull in with a bunch of cows that lived around where we were. They didn't have to stay there, there were no fences, they had 35,000 acres to roam in, but they'd chosen this as their patch.

This Brahman bull was a wild-eyed, tilt-horned, dangerous looking hunk of work with a big hump on his shoulders.

"Just keep out of his way," advised the stockman. "He'll settle down when he's been here for a while."

Whenever we came within two hundred yards of the bull he'd stand up and snort and dig up the ground with his front feet and stare at us with a disquieting intensity. We would discreetly move away from there.

That bull and I gradually got a thing going. He and his cows were camped on a big tussock terrace about a thousand feet above the river. In the evenings I used to stroll around there and sit on the side of the hill and have a smoke, just at the edge of the bull's range of agitation, ignoring him. He'd keep an eye on me, but bit by bit I got closer and closer before he let me know that that was close enough.

In the finish I could stroll casually to within sixty yards of him, careful not to look directly at him, and squat down and roll a smoke, looking out over the valley, and if he and his cows were lying down he wouldn't even get up. I'd finish my smoke and stand up and stroll away, stopping to look around the scenery every now and then. Cool.

Then one evening I was sitting fifty yards from him, the closest I'd ever been. He and his cows were all lying down and I could see out the corner of my eye that he was chewing his cud. No worries there. The last traces of sunlight were fading from the top of Mount Gilbert. Not a breath of wind. The valley was still and silent. The mountains were turning slowly purple with the encroaching dusk.

This tranquil scene was suddenly shattered in a most dramatic way. It started when I got a big wet kiss on the back of the neck. I knew no one was there. I know that men aren't supposed to scream, but this one screamed that time. I leapt up and spun round and saw two things. The first thing I saw was that a prospector's old dog we were looking after had left the camp and wandered after me and stuck its nose in the back of my neck.

The other thing I saw was that the Brahman bull was coming at me, flat-tack with its head down. He was no more than twenty-five yards from me. There was no time to think about this. I turned and jumped straight over the edge onto a steep slip of stones and matagouri and rolled and scrambled and tumbled down the hill. It was where the miners had sluiced down the hillside in the old days and it was all steep bare stones. Stones were coming down after me, which I thought were being dislodged by the bull.

I reached the bottom. Rocks were still rolling down the slip but they were only ones I'd dislodged myself. The bull was nowhere in sight, he'd evidently stopped at the top, which was just as well for me because I was so knocked around I couldn't have run anywhere. I'd sprained an ankle, cracked an elbow, split my scalp and lost a fair bit of hide off various parts of me.

I hobbled down to a track that followed the river and, with the aid of a stick, made it down the river and up a track to the hut, the last bit in the dark. I had to yell out to my wife what had happened before I came into the light in case she got too much of a fright when she saw me.

I was out of action for two weeks, and after that we couldn't go within four hundred yards of the Brahman bull without him starting to run round and snort and paw the ground. He didn't trust us any more. This was highly inconvenient to us because it cut us off from access to a big hunk of our claim and the best way to get up to our hut from the river. We were getting around keeping a sharp lookout for wild animals, like they did in Neolithic times.

One day my wife was riding back into the claim leading the packhorse with a load of supplies. She was nearly there when she suddenly found that she'd ridden between the Brahman bull and his cows. And he wasn't happy about it. He charged and stopped short of her and then ran across to his cows, snorting and carrying on. It sounds like he was bluffing, but the pack-horse panicked and pulled away from her and bolted back along the track towards town.

She had to follow it for about an hour along the narrow trail before she could get past and catch the packhorse. When she got back to where the bull had been it was gone. She arrived at the hut late and hacked off. All the candles and eggs were broken from being jolted around on the packhorse. Omelette for dinner that night, and breakfast the next morning. Omelette for lunch, and then no eggs for a fortnight.

After that incident my wife was a bit nervous of going anywhere round there on her own, but then we got one back on the Brahman bull. We'd both been out for supplies and didn't run into any bulls. We'd bought a mineral salt-block for the horses and it was on the ground outside the hut.

There must have been a severe salt deficiency in that area. We'd been told by the musterers that the stock would travel surprising distances and even bust through fences to get at a salt lick. Our horses chewed and slobbered at it and ate the corners off it before they'd had enough and wandered off. We left the block there in case they wanted more later.

We heard something out there in the night and thought it must have been the horses. I got up at daylight and looked out the window and saw the Brahman bull and two of his cows blissfully slurping away at the mineral block. I whispered to my wife to get up and watch this. Then I suddenly flung open the hut door and yelled YAAAAAH!

His Nibs got such a fright that he bolted straight ahead and blundered right through the woodshed. Wrecked it. Then he got tangled in wire trying to get out through the horse-paddock fence and ended up sprawling and rolling down a steep hill into swamp, which he had a bit of trouble getting out of. He never was much good on rough going, must have come from where it was flat. The last we saw of the Brahman bull that time he was mooching away around the mountainside, muddy and limping, driven from the battle by a second scream. We were square.

Not long after that he took his cows away up a side valley and we had the place to ourselves again.

There's an interesting ending to the story of the Brahman bull. By the time he'd been on the place for six months and they'd had him in the yards a couple of times, he'd settled right down. He even looked at you different. You could chase him out of the way on foot. He was more shy than anything else, though they still had to watch him in the yards if he started getting snorty.

The reason the Brahman bull had been so toey when he first came amongst us was probably because he'd been suddenly chased into a yard, shunted onto a truck and dogged and driven away from everything he'd ever known and dumped into a completely strange environment.

I'd say that'd be enough to cause any self-respecting Brahman bull to object to being snuck up on and screamed at, wouldn't you?

GOLD FEVER

MY WIFE AND I had a gold claim where quite a few recreational gold-miners used to come to try their luck. We sometimes lent people a gold pan and shovel and told them where to dig, and it was a pleasure to see their faces when they got a few flakes of gold in their pan.

It's a fascinating thing, panning gold, and sometimes people become afflicted with what's known as gold fever, and that can be funny to watch.

We were putting river shingle through a large riffle-box with a front-end loader one day and we'd stopped for a brew of tea when four people, two middle-aged couples, doctors and their wives, came along the track that followed the creek we were working in. We starting talking about gold and my wife got a pan and shovel and took the two women over to the edge of the creek to show them how to do it.

The men and I were talking away when there were some excited squeals from the women and they came running over to show us several flakes of gold in the gold pan. My wife and I knew there was gold there but you'd think these women had made a major strike, especially one of them.

I put the flakes in a small glass bottle for them, and by the time I'd done that one of the women was back in the creek, energetically panning all wrong. My wife went and helped her get it right and I made the others a cup of tea.

The men were apologising for holding us up, I was telling them it was okay, the other wife was having trouble with the sandflies and the gold fever one was head down in the creek, wet to the armpits, oblivious of the sandflies, digging panfuls of gravel from further out in the creek to see if there was more gold there.

They approached her several times saying they really ought to get away but there was no shifting her. She was getting a few flakes in her bottle and just wanted to try this other place over here.

My wife and I decided to wash up our riffle-box and lifted it out of the creek and took the riffles out of it and washed the gravel and black sand into a pan and put it through a small riffle-box in the creek. The gold fever lady knocked off to come over and watch the final wash-up. We had about a third of an ounce of gold in the pan, including several small nuggets. The gold fever lady poked it and shook it around in the pan, hypnotised by it, and when we added it to a jar that already had about three ounces of gold in it she lost all semblance of dignity. She grabbed her pan and shovel and dived back into the creek. If we could get gold like that, so could she.

My wife and I wanted to do some work on a garden we were putting in so we left them there and went up the hill to our hut.

The next morning when we went down to the claim the first thing we noticed was the gold fever lady's bum. She was panning gravel from the hole I'd been digging with the loader the day before. Her long-suffering husband was sitting on the bank, reading a newspaper and drinking tea from a thermos cup. The other couple had gone jet-boating for the day.

We told the gold fever lady she'd do better along the bank we'd put her onto the day before, but she had gold fever, she'd gone suspicious. Why would a gold-miner tell another gold-miner where the best place for gold was? We tried to explain how much material we'd had to put through the riffle-box to get that gold, but we had to agree that she could quite possibly find a rich patch of flakes or a nugget with her pan and shovel. There was no way of telling her what the odds were, she had gold fever.

It's amazing how quickly people smitten with gold fever become experts. While we were eating lunch the gold fever lady pointed out a bend of the creek where, she said, there were probably layers of gold thrown up by the floods. We'd prospected that bend, there was nothing in it.

We got about another third of an ounce that day. The long-suffering husband helped my wife keep the stuff moving through the riffle-box and the gold fever lady got enough flakes to cover the bottom of her bottle, maybe half a pennyweight, about seven dollars worth. She'd lost track of how hard she'd worked to get it, it was gold and she'd found it all by herself.

We took the gold fever lady and the long-suffering husband up to our hut and showed them some gold and ended up selling them an ounce of it, including quite a nice nugget we'd found. They were a pleasant couple and we enjoyed their company, except that she could talk about nothing but gold.

They turned up every day for the next few days and the gold fever lady got about the same amount of gold each day, nearly none. Then one morning when we arrived at the claim the gold fever lady and the long-suffering husband were standing with their backs to us as we approached, having an argument. The long-suffering husband had had enough. We heard him saying, ". . . only had a week and you've spent five bloody days of it arse up in a bloody creek looking for bloody gold, and you haven't found enough of the bloody stuff to fill the holes in your bloody teeth!"

I dropped a gold pan and they heard it and switched off. The long-suffering husband explained that they'd only come in that day to say goodbye and thank us for all the help we'd given them, but by the time he'd finished telling us that the gold fever lady was back in the creek, panning for gold.

The long-suffering husband tried to be nice about it and then got progressively less nice, but he couldn't get his wife out of that creek She just wanted to do this one other pan. Finally the long-suffering husband lost his rag. We could hear him over the sound of the loader.

"Well I'm bloody going," he shouted. "And if you don't bloody want to come you can bloody well stay here!" and he stalked off along the track towards where their car was parked.

With great reluctance the gold fever lady put the pan and shovel on the bank and waved to us and dragged her feet off along the track after her long-suffering husband, with her pathetic bit of gold in her bottle.

It could wreck a marriage, that gold fever.

A mate of ours has had gold fever for years. He was always turning up with new and revolutionary gold recovery gear. Pumps and diggers, suction dredges and detectors, new types of riffles and once, to his great embarrassment, a gold-divining rod he'd sent away for. All this equipment was employed in pursuit of Fred's burning ambition, to find a big nugget. Every weekend and holiday for years he burrowed and scavenged in the creeks and river banks in search of his big nugget. He found quite a bit of gold but nothing much bigger than the head of a four-inch nail. We used to tease him about it.

One of the symptoms of gold fever is that the enthusiasm of the sufferer is inexhaustible, it never wanes. Fred tried every new method and followed up every new theory or rumour with an enthusiasm completely unimpaired by years of failure.

One day my wife and I found a big nugget in our riffle-box. It was a beaut. Over an ounce in weight. A big piece of gold for that region, or any other for that matter.

We took a photograph of the nugget beside a matchbox in a gold pan and sent it to Fred, along with a letter telling him we'd come by this nugget in the strangest way, and that it was called the 'Nugget of the Tattooed Leg'.

Fred, in the relentless grip of gold fever, smelt a mystery and couldn't resist writing back and asking some not-very-subtle questions about where and how we'd got the nugget, and why it was called the Nugget of the Tattooed Leg. We decided that the joke had gone far enough. This was my reply to his letter:

Dear Fred,
Your letter is to hand and we rejoice to learn that you
    continue to enjoy good health and prosperity.
Our lives have been in something of a turmoil since we
    acquired the Nugget of the Tattooed Leg. As a miner
    yourself from way back you will know that gold is
    strange stuff and causes people to do strange things. I
    know you will understand the strange circumstances by
    which this nugget came into our possession.
I was in Queenstown one night a few weeks back, hastening
    to an assignation with a Nepalese drug dealer. The
    directions I'd been given took me through the Haitian
    quarter and, glancing around at the squalid hovels of this
    crowded sprawling slum, I shuddered and raised my coat
    collar against the clammy late-night mist and hurried on
    my way, anxious to do my business and be away from
    this unwholesome place.
Suddenly, up ahead of me on a dimly-lit street corner, I saw
    three men attacking another. I immediately ran to his
    assistance and, by the use of some karate skills I'd
    learned while tea planting on the Chathams, I managed
    to fend off the three huge Negro attackers, who finally
    gave up and ran off into the darkness.

195

Turning for the first time to the man I'd saved I saw that he
was an old Chinese gentleman, lying in a crumpled heap
on the littered roadway. He appeared to be badly hurt. I
gently lifted him up and carried him into a nearby hovel
and laid him on an evil-smelling couch of uncured
goatskins, and ordered the trembling Vietnamese boat-
people occupants to bring towels and hot water.

By the dim light of a flickering lamp I removed the old man's
torn shirt and washed him. He was badly bruised and
had several knife cuts about his body and had lost a lot
of blood. I cleaned his wounds and staunched them with
bandages improvised from a sarong torn into strips.
Then I forced a few drops of Fanta between his clenched
gums and laid him back on the couch and covered him
with a dog-skin blanket. After a while the Fanta began to
take its effect and the poor old man drifted off into a
troubled sleep.

I sat with him through the long night, mopping the sweat
from his fevered brow and checking his pulse and
breathing. Towards morning he awoke and began
mumbling feverishly. I bent closer to try to hear what he
was going on about and distinctly heard him say "gold"
and "map".

Gold and map – at the mention of those magic words I
underwent a transformation, from a decent bloke doing
another bloke a favour, to a miserable, mercenary,
materialistic misanthropist.

I shook him. "What gold?" I said urgently.

"Gold," he muttered. "Big gold."

"Where?" I demanded.

"Map," he gasped, and fell weakly back against the sack of
mussels I'd given him for a pillow.

I shook him again. "Where's the map?" I said.

"Leg," he muttered. "On leg."

I threw aside the dog-skin blanket and slit his trouser leg with my knife and held the lamp closer, and there on the calf of his leg was a faded tattoo, a map giving directions to a spot in a creek deep in the Gore Mountains.

Taking the leg with me, I made my way back to my camp, and the next day I trekked into the mountains with my faithful burro and prospecting equipment. Following the directions on the leg I picked my way through gorge and gully until, on the third day, I came to the spot marked on the leg.

I noticed a pile of stones that had once been built up into a cairn, so I dug there and to my horror unearthed a human skeleton in a shallow grave. The skull had been crushed in, telling of some grisly deed perpetrated in the purple past.

"Probably over gold," I mused to myself, and just then I saw the gleam of gold among the bones of the skeleton's hand. It was the nugget that has come to be called the Nugget of the Tattooed Leg. I grabbed it and after gazing upon it for a while I put it in my pocket and then threw the bones aside and put the whole area through my riffle-box. But not another speck of gold did I find.

I could have murdered that old Chink. He'd put me crook, made me go to all that trouble for one lousy nugget. But it just goes to show you what men will do for "the muck called gold".

I'm happy to be able to report however that some good has come from that experience. Maggie and I have decided to shut ourselves away in the Ben Lomond shearers' quarters and spend our declining years working on a cure for gold fever. Doctor Crump's Famous Gold Fever Pills!

At the moment we're working on a mixture of sandfly bites,

wet arses, numb fingers and nothing in the wash-up. If
we can get that into a pill we feel that we will have made
a break-through in the search for a remedy for this most
degrading of human afflictions.

Who knows what it might lead to? One of them Nobel prizes
wouldn't go astray, or a seat on the Board (I've always
wanted one of those), or maybe even an interview on the
telly!

But enough of this silly day-dreaming, I must away and give
Maggie a hand. She's having trouble getting the
flavouring right. We've decided on a sardine-on-toast
flavour for our pills.

So until we next meet, our warmest regards.

Crumpy.

P.S. You didn't think we'd tell you where we really got it, did
you?

Fred's reply said simply, You bastards!

A DAY WITH UNC

M Y WIFE AND I were camping in a horse float on the Hokianga Harbour, netting flounder for a crust, when we crossed paths with the most unhurried bloke I ever came across. They called him Unc, short for Unconscious. We never found out what his real name was. He was a short, round Maori bloke, about forty-five, and he was so slow that stories were made up about him.

Some young kids told us in all seriousness that Unc had an extra-slow heartbeat and everyone had to wait for him. He was born in a leap year and it took him four years to do what everyone else did in one year. His hair and fingernails, they assured us, grew slower than everyone else's and he only needed a haircut every six months. The things people let their kids believe!

You couldn't blame the kids for believing some of that stuff. Unc was so incredibly slow, he even thought slow. He couldn't keep up with an ordinary conversation, he'd say something about something that had already been said and you'd have to think back to remember what it was. He wasn't dumb, just slow. It took him a whole day to read a comic. He must have been hell on his teachers at school.

Before we got to know him properly my wife and I agreed to go with Unc one day and give him a hand to load some posts onto a trailer and take them up to the marae. It was a job that should have taken about an hour, two hours at the most, three would have been ridiculous. It took all day.

For a start Unc didn't turn up where we were supposed to

meet him. We waited about half an hour for him and then drove to his place to see what was holding him up, but we missed him because he'd gone round the other way to pick up the trailer. It took us another half hour to find him. We parked our ute on the side of the road and got into his cousin's old car with him and off we went to get this load of posts.

We thought Unc knew where he was going, he told us he'd been there before, but now he wasn't quite sure which place it was. He pulled into a driveway that turned out to be the wrong one and we had to unhitch the trailer and drag it out into the paddock so he could turn the car around and then hook it on again.

Half the problem was that Unc couldn't remember anyone's name quick enough. He called everyone What's-his-name, even if he'd known them for years. What we'd undertaken to do that day was "take Wassname's trailer up to Wassname's place and get some posts for the wassname."

I finally got a name off him and directions from four young kids riding past on a horse, and we found Wassname's place. Mr and Mrs Wassname were just about to have a bit of morning tea when we arrived and we had to join them for smoked eel and damper with mugs of milky tea. The Wassnames weren't in any great hurry to get on with anything either and it was another hour before we got the trailer backed up to a stack of posts in their paddock.

"How many of these do you want, Unc?" I asked him, picking up a post and throwing it onto the trailer.

"Six," said Unc.

My wife and I looked at each other. Unc had brought us out here to help him load six posts onto a trailer?

"Six?" I said.

"Yeah, but they have to be the right ones."

"What do you mean?"

"They want two big ones and four small ones."

By the time we'd sorted out the right six posts and loaded them onto the trailer another half an hour had elapsed, and then we discovered that one of the trailer tyres was almost flat and the other was half-flat. We weren't going to get far with it like that so we unloaded the posts and crawled into Opononi at five miles an hour. While I pumped up the trailer tyres Unc was side-tracked by two of his cousins, both called Wassname, who had a fishing boat berthed at the wharf just there. They invited us on board for a feed of mussels they were just cooking up.

We'd set off at eight o'clock that morning to give Unc a hand for an hour and here we were at lunchtime sitting on a boat eating shellfish and bread, two-and-a-half miles further away from the posts than when we'd set off.

After lunch, which took another hour or so, we took leave of our hosts and got in the car and drove back to Wassname's place to get the posts. At least we knew where we were going this time and which posts we wanted, so some progress had been made. We got the posts loaded back onto the trailer without any further diversions, but as we drove out past the Wassnames' house they waved us down and called out for us to come in and have a kai of pig's head and puha.

Despite the fact that we were already full of seafood, to pass up a feed of pig's head and puha was apparently unthinkable, not to say possibly insulting, so it was back round the Wassnames' kitchen table. It was a good kai too, and it was yet another hour before we were back in the car, groaning with fullness, heading for the wassname with our six posts on the trailer.

We came up the hill to the marae, where two blokes, called Wassname and Wassname, were hanging a gate at the entrance. The new fence around the marae was finished. Unc had been too slow even for them and they'd scrounged the extra posts they needed two days before. It was a good thing we'd turned up, though. They'd sent the wrong-sized gate and someone had to take it into Kaikohe and change it for the right one.

I thought that might let us off this drawn-out business of Unc's posts, but no such luck. There were problems. Like none of them had a driver's licence, neither the car nor the trailer were registered or had Warrants of Fitness and it was a bit dangerous to take them into town. There also seemed to be some doubt about whether they could rake up enough money for the gas. There was a big official function on at the marae the next day and the fence was supposed to be finished.

After having enjoyed such lavish hospitality from the locals all day what else could we do? We loaded the wrong-sized gate onto the trailer and took it to our ute and drove them to Kaikohe and got the right-sized gate and returned to the marae with it.

It was getting on in the day by the time we'd given the Wassnames a hand to hang the right-sized gate and taken the latch off the post and put it on in the right place, and it was getting dark when we dropped Unc off at the car with the posts on the trailer. No worries, he could drop the posts back to Wassnames' tomorrow. Thanks for giving him a hand with them.

"Wouldn't have missed it for quids, Unc."

He was blithely satisfied that he'd put in a decent day's work. Quite unaware that he'd caused more work than he'd got done, and it still wasn't finished. It would probably take him all the next day to return those posts.

That night, as we cleared our flounder net by torchlight, we marvelled at the slowness of Unc and swore in the interests of our sanity never to get caught up in his languid pace ever again. It was too hectic for us.

"I wonder what makes him like that?" said my wife.

"I don't know," I said, "but those Wassnames weren't much faster than Unc himself. Maybe it's environmental round here."

"Well I hope it's not contagious," joked my wife.

But it turned out to be no joke. The day with Unc had proved very contagious indeed. We started calling people and places and things we couldn't think of the name of 'Wassname', and in spite of conscious efforts to cut it out we were still doing it long after we left Hokianga. In fact I still slip into it now and again. He was a nice enough bloke, Wassname, but I'm glad we weren't stuck with him for a whole week.

CLIVE'S GOATS

A FEW YEARS back I was fencing and breaking in a block of scrubby overgrown land on an abandoned sheep station up a valley in Hawke's Bay. I'd been slogging away at it for about a year and beginning to be able to see where I'd been when my neighbour sold off a fifteen-acre block of land, a lifestyle block, right up against my boundary. There was a dilapidated old two-bedroomed farm cottage and a corrugated-iron carshed on the place, and a driveway that was always washed out.

The first lot of people who had the place were a bunch of recycled hippies who always seemed to be sitting around talking about what they were going to do. They were into gardening and within a year they'd been busted by the police for growing the wrong kind of vegetable matter, and evicted from the place for not having paid for it. They left behind them a hell of a mess, including the shell of an old Bedford house-bus they hadn't been able to get up the driveway to the house. It was already becoming engulfed in long grass and blackberry vines on the side of the road.

The next owners of the lifestyle block were a bloke called Clive Piper and his wife Maisy, who'd sold a milk bar and dairy in Hamilton and moved out into the country to bring up their two kids in 'a healthy environment'. They were a likeable young couple, keen as mustard, but they didn't have much idea of how to go about things in the country. They had an Alsatian dog and a couple of cats, and they bought a horse off a Maori bloke out at the turn-off up our road. The horse was always getting out of their one paddock and wandering up the road to my place, mainly because they kept forgetting to keep their gate shut, and I'd have to round it up for them.

Clive was up at my place quite a bit, asking advice about one thing and another, and I was down at their place quite a bit, digging a hole with the tractor for all the rubbish left behind by the previous tenants, fixing the driveway every time we had a bit of heavy rain, cutting racks of firewood for them, and shaking my head about what they should do with their fifteen acres of blackberry, ragwort, thistles, fern, bulrushes and rank grass.

Like all lifestyle blocks it was too small to make a living off in that kind of country. No good for horticulture or cropping, too small for farming enough sheep or cattle and too big to keep from growing into weeds. All I could suggest was that they either spray it or mow it.

They had some money to keep them going until they could find some way of making a living there but I didn't like their chances. Then Clive got this idea and came up to my place to tell me about it.

"Goats, Crumpy," he said enthusiastically. "Angora goats! I've been reading up on it. There's a big demand worldwide for angora fibre. All you have to do is get an angora billygoat and a flock of feral goats and breed from them until you get angora wool. It's worth more than twice as much as sheep wool!"

I was sceptical but I didn't like to knock him back too much.

"You'd have to do something about your boundary fence if you want to keep goats in," I told him.

All his boundary fence, except where he adjoined my place, was about eighty years old. I knew what it was like because I'd had to pull some of it down. Totara posts you could snap off at the ground with one jerk, with a few strands of rusty number-eight and barbed wire. A goat would have walked straight through it just about anywhere.

I gave him a couple of my days and we set about replacing posts with treated pine and stapling new rolls of goat-netting onto it. Then Clive arrived home with a purebred long-horned angora billygoat he'd got from a stud farm near Kawhia. He'd paid nine thousand dollars for it. It was called Basil, papers and all. The price he'd paid for the thing shook me somewhat.

Basil was very tame and, quite frankly, a blasted nuisance. He didn't like children (I was going to say kids) and they couldn't go into the paddock with him unless they were escorted by an adult. He'd charge up and bowl them. He dragged Maisy's washing down off the clothesline and chewed it. He'd eat anything in a bucket he could get at, whether it was clothes, pegs, potato peelings, scraps, paper, plastic, rubber or wood, and if there was nothing in the bucket he'd chew the bucket itself. He even got stuck into some waste oil Clive had drained out of his ute. It's a wonder Basil didn't do himself a mischief, the things he ingested. Their Alsatian dog was scared of Basil. I offered to give him a shake-up with my dogs but Clive wouldn't let me. Basil was much too valuable an animal for anything like that.

Then Clive bought forty feral goats they'd rounded up off the hills behind Gisborne. I went down with him to collect them and we brought them back in two trailers. They were a miserable wormy-looking lot, all the colours of the rainbow and a few more, like khaki and ginger. He'd paid a hundred and fifty dollars each for them. Two of them died in the trailer on the way home.

We let the goats off the trailers into Clive's paddock and went inside for a cup of tea, and when I came out to go home one of the new goats was standing on top of a strainer post we'd put in the top corner of Clive's boundary. A brown and white one. Clive was a bit dismayed by this.

"What are we going to do about that, Crumpy?"

"Well for a start I'd shoot that one for dog tucker, if I were you," I told him. "You'll never keep that goat in here. It'll end up getting away into the bush and probably take a few of the others with it. You'd better shoot the thing."

He reluctantly agreed, but I had to do it for him. Clive couldn't bear to do things like that.

Within a week six goats had got out over the netting and disappeared through the fern and scrub into the bush above Clive's place. Two of them came out at the top of my place and I caught them with the dogs and threw them over the fence into the paddock, but within a couple of days they'd escaped into the bush again.

Then some of Clive's goats developed contagious footrot, which quickly began to spread among them. We put them in the trailer and took them up to my yards in batches and put them through a footbath of zinc-sulphate. That had to be done several times to clear the flock of footrot. In the meantime my sheep had picked it up and had to be done as well.

Then some of the goats started dying on him. We took them up to my yards again and drenched them. That fixed the problem, but the survivors became very active and wild. One day nearly all of them got out through a hole that had washed out under the fence. Clive came up to my place in a state of great agitation and I went down there with the dogs and managed to round them all up and drive them down a creek and up his driveway and back into the paddock. Then we found the hole in the fence and fixed it.

Twenty-eight of Clive's goats survived to produce kids, thirty-six of them, all white. Basil had done something right. One more generation and Clive would be able to start selling the fleeces off them.

By this time the goats were making some impression on

the weeds on his place. In fact he was getting short of feed for them and they were getting harder to keep in. He had to start buying bags of goat-pellets for them, a very costly thing to have to do. I tried to persuade him to cull out some of the male goats and some of the feral nannies but it was too late. They'd been getting very tame since they'd started hand-feeding them and they'd got fond of the things. Maisy had given them all names and couldn't bear to part with any of them. Everywhere she went she was knee-deep in goats, all clamouring for a feed of goat nuts. She believed it was because they loved her, but they'd have cheerfully trodden her to death in the mud to get at a pocketful of goat nuts.

"Maisy'd never let me sell any of her goats, Crumpy," said Clive seriously.

We built Clive and Maisy a small set of yards and they fed the goats in them, which made them much easier to manage. They had to be drenched and have their feet clipped once a month, another thing I had to show them how to do. I was spending almost as much time on Clive's goats as I was on my place, and I wasn't convinced that it was ever going to be worth it.

I'd suggested that Clive change his breeding billygoat but he assured me it wasn't necessary. You could put an angora billygoat to his daughters, it said so in *Breeding Angora Goats in New Zealand.* But in spite of that Basil's second generation of offspring turned out to be weak and weedy. You'd hardly have got enough fibre from a fleece off one of them to make a hat for a hen. He'd wasted a whole breeding year.

At about this time we learned that the bottom had fallen right out of the angora goat-fibre market. There was little demand for it any more. An oversupply worldwide. It was hardly worth taking the fleece off a full-grown one, let along something the size of a large hare. Clive was ruined, ruined by goats. He confided to me that they'd cost him twenty-three thousand dollars, and he hadn't made a single buck out of them. He finally had to acknowledge that the goats were a lost cause.

"What's the best thing to do with them, Crumpy?" he pleaded.

"Get rid of them," I said. "Sell them for whatever you can get for them."

"I might get a bit of my money back for Basil," he said hopefully. "He's a pedigree animal."

But Basil beat him to it. He died from consuming half a bucketful of post staples. Clive sold the rest of his flock to a buyer for weed-control on a property down the coast. He got six dollars each for them.

Clive and Maisy had been in the valley for three years and Maisy was getting burnt out from having to drive the kids fifteen Ks along the twisting country road to the nearest school-bus corner every morning and pick them up again in the afternoons. She'd had enough of it. There was no way Clive was ever going to get work around there, there just wasn't any. They decided to move back to town. I was going to miss them, but I sure as hell wasn't going to miss Clive's goats.

By the time I sold up and left that valley the lifestyle block was still unsold and growing back again into blackberry, ragwort, thistles, fern, bulrushes and rank grass. The only reminder of Clive's goats was Basil's horns left hanging on the fence.

LETTER TO THE I.R.D.

A WHILE BACK I was living on the outskirts of what might be described as a one-horse town. One road, one store, one garage, one policeman, one bank, one school, one church, two pubs and three hundred people. I was friendly with the couple who ran the top pub and used to help out behind the bar when they were busy or had to go down to the city for something. It's hard to get away when you run a country pub.

One morning I did the bar for them while Bert and Rene visited friends of theirs who had a farm not far out of town. I was going on a hunting trip that afternoon and needed some folding to buy supplies from the store, so I wrote out a cash cheque for sixty dollars and stuck it in the till and took out the money, bought my supplies and left for the bush as soon as Bert and Rene arrived back.

I was away for three weeks and when I returned to the village it was a long weekend and there were a fair few campers, trampers, trout-fisherpersons and other holiday-makers around. The pub was quite busy and I got behind the bar to take a bit of weight off Bert, who was inclined to get slower the busier it got.

One of the locals borrowed a pen and wrote out a cheque and when I went to slip it under the twenties in the till, where we put the cheques, I saw my sixty-dollar cheque in there, looking a bit creased and grubby. It should have been banked long before this. I took it out and had a look at it, to make sure

210

I'd written it out properly, and discovered a curious thing. There was writing on the back of it that told the story of its travels since I'd put it in there.

Bert had paid Herbie Wilson, the carrier, with it for cartage of the kegs of beer and stuff. Then Herbie had given it to Mike Turner at the garage in payment for gas. Mike had then given it to Jack Palmer at the store for groceries. Jack had paid Big Andy Pratt with it for cutting his grass, and Andy had given it to the publican down at the Commercial for his bar bill, and the publican had used it to pay two blokes who'd painted a fence for him. They must have come in and cashed it with Bert, and here it was back in his till.

We were fairly busy and I didn't have time to work out how all that had happened. I was going to need some cash myself, so I stuck the sixty-dollar cheque in my pocket and wrote out another one for a hundred dollars, put it in the till and took out forty dollars. I was square with the till.

Later, when I found the sixty-dollar cheque among the other stuff I had on me, I tried to figure out how it had paid all those people and then ended back in my pocket. All the recipients had obviously been satisfied with it, and yet it had never been in the bank.

I decided to have a yarn with Bert about it, he knows how the system works from having been in business all his life.

"You're supposed to declare all your income so they can tax you on it," he said.

I pointed out that I'd got that money from possum skins I'd trapped and I'd already paid twenty-five cents in the dollar tax on it, which actually made it three-quarters of eighty dollars. If the others had all had to pay the same on it we'd have had to find another sixty dollars just to pay the tax.

"That makes it a hundred and twenty dollars tax on sixty dollars," I said.

"That's not how it works," said Bert.

"I don't see how it can work at all," I said. "If you and Herbie and Mike and Jack had paid tax on that cheque it would have been all gone before it got to Big Andy, and here it is, paid another four people and come back to me, still worth sixty bucks."

"You've still got to pay your tax," Bert insisted.

"But I pay tax every time I buy petrol, food, beer, smokes, clothes – everything I buy I pay tax," I said.

"You always have to pay tax," he said philosophically. "It's a fact of life."

"Does the government pay tax on all the tax they get?" I asked him.

"I don't know," he stammered. "I suppose it does."

"Who do they pay it to?" I wanted to know.

"Inland Revenue, I suppose."

"Where does it go from there?"

"Back to the government of course."

"Then how come the government hasn't already got all the money there is around?" I asked him.

That shook him. He had no reply.

"You still have to pay your tax," he said weakly. "It's a fact of life."

"It's a fact that this cheque has paid five hundred and forty dollars' worth of bills and ended up back where it started," I said, waving it at him.

He was stonkered, I'd shot his argument down in flames. My cheque had done the rounds without any processing or handling charges or overheads. No G.S.T. or I.R.D. numbers, no statements, accounts or receipts, no deposit slips or withdrawal forms, no waiting for clearance of the cheque or standing in queues in banks. Without so much as a handshake my sixty-dollar cheque had flowed smoothly through all those transactions without a single hitch or delay.

It looks to me as though we're onto something here. I hope I'm not turning into a communist or Social Creditor or anything. It's not my intention to stir up sedition or bring the elected government of the land undone, but I reckon I've stumbled onto a better system of running the financial affairs of society than the one they've been using. What do you reckon?

There's a sequel to the story of the sixty-dollar cheque. About a month after I'd stuck it on a nail in the wall of my hut I received a letter from the Inland Revenue Department, informing me that they had no record of having received a tax return from me, nor did I seem to have any I.R.D. number. They seemed rather unhappy about this, so to cheer up the poor chap who'd written the letter I sent this poem in reply:

Dear Sir,
Your letter says – my conscience burns!
    – I've never furnished tax returns.
And, furthermore, you seem to say, it's getting too late anyway.
And, further-furthermore, you add, the situation's very bad,
And if I don't, by yesterday, produce returns
    – there's hell to pay!

No problem, sir, we'll put that right;
    I'll write it down this very night;
Employers, dates, in each detail
    – we'll sort this whole thing out by mail!
You see, I've kept a careful track of everything,
        for income-tack,
And saved it for this very day. Coincidental, sir? – I'll say!
So with respect for you and me, I won't put on false modesty.
I'll just stick down the simple fax of you and me,
        and income tax.

I left home, sir, at an early age and went in search of work and
      wage
And got a job repairing sacks, so I could pay some income tax.

I didn't know that from the start the firm was shaky – fell apart,
And by the time I'd paid the boss, I stood a quite substantial
      loss.
I learned to cook and did so well they made me chef at Brent's
      Hotel.
The fat caught fire, the pub burnt down and, broke, I had to
      leave the town.

At trading I was doing well, I couldn't get enough to sell.
My profits vanished – every cent – the victim of embezzlement.
I then moved on to other things, to seek the revenue they brings,
But one by one my ventures failed and constant losses were
      entailed.

For instance in the timber trade I really thought I had it made,
Until they went and 'sent me through', to cheat the Inland
      Revenue!
You know yourself how these things are – I had some trouble
      with my car
Then mortgage people haunted me and drove me into
      bankruptcy.

And so the years have drifted by; regardless of how hard I try
(You might just call it rotten luck) I haven't made a single buck.
But I didn't need to stay at school to get good at mini-pool,
Or learn that life gives nothing free, it's what you make it, you
      and me.

Take me, now, who'd have ever guessed I'd end up too poor to
    invest
In things like inland revenue – I think it's rather sad, don't you?
But when it comes to golf, old chap, I'm on a seven handicap
And, yes, (how sharp of you to guess!) I play a decent game of
    chess.

I know what won the Melbourne Cup and what's the score in
    Bangladup.
I'll rattle off the All Black team and tell you what it should have
    been.
I know the current price of gold and just what shares were
    bought and sold;
I've heard the joke you'll tell tonight – I guess you'd say I'm
    pretty bright.

But when it comes to currency the blasted stuff just dodges me.
I tell you, sir, I've had a lash at handling everything but cash!
And so, old friend, my point is made, I give these details
    unafraid.
And when you come to judge my case you'll feel the same as
    me, Your Grace.

But please don't think it's been in vain – I know I'll soon come
    right again,
For after all it isn't *who,* it's *what* you know that gets you
    through.
And meantime, sir, may I suggest a way to meet the problem
    best –
Relying on our mutual trust, *you* pay the tax for both of us.

And then when things come right for me I'll do the same for you,
    you see?

215

It's one of nature's basic laws – you pay my tax, I'll pay yours!
And one day, when I'm all cashed up, I'll come to town and look
    you up.
No, really sir, I can't be rude, I'll *have t*o show my gratitude.

And when we're back to square again and everything's as right as
    rain,
We'll have the whole thing sorted out and no, sir, it'll be *my* shout.
And won't we chuckle when we see how close we've grown, sir,
    you and me.
The bonds of friendship, forged on facts of you, and me, and
    income tax!

Just one last thing before I go, you'll understand, Your Grace, I
    know.
I wouldn't need a large amount, let's just say fifty, on account.
The going's been a little tough, but fifty bucks should be enough.
A money-order telegram? I can't say, sir, how pleased I am!

And any time you need advice, just call on me, sir, don't think
    twice.
I wouldn't put you crook, you'll see — we'll be good mates, sir,
    you and me!
I trust you, sir, no need to say you'll send the fifty right away.
Don't worry, sir, you'll get it back, see ya, cobber, Your Friend,
    Jack.

I eagerly await his reply.

ANACHRONOLOGY

ANACHRONOLOGY IS A word I've been forced to coin in order to describe a disconcerting condition I suffer from. It describes the state of being out-of-date. You see, I was born thirty years later than I should have been. I only began to realise that I was afflicted with this disturbing malady when I tried to adjust a digital watch someone had given me. I ended up with it hopelessly out of time and the date wrong and in French and an alarm that kept going off all the time. Then, just to rub it in, my seven-year-old nipper gave it a few flicks and twists and had it adjusted right in no time at all, and then commandeered it for his trouble. Makes a man feel a bit anachronistic, a thing like that.

Then there was the radio in a car I bought. In my day radios had knobs, two of them. You turned one knob to switch it on and adjust the volume, and the other knob was for changing the station. Not so with these modern jobs. This one had AM, FM, mono, treb, bass, scan, bal, tun, and flickering lights and flashing numbers. I never got the hang of it and left it on the one station I found until I sold the car.

My family claimed I was depriving them because we didn't have a video recorder, so one day I bought one, and had to wait for the kids to come home from school to hook it up to the television set. I never got the hang of that thing either. It's too complicated for me. If I want to record a programme I have to get someone to set it up for me, but I can turn the telly on and off and change channels with the remote control thing.

"You're behind the times, Crumpy," they said to me. "You want to chuck that old chequebook away and get yourself a credit card. It's much easier and simpler and safer."

For all I knew they were right. I didn't want to fall too far behind the times. I was already becoming concerned about my ability to cope in a technological society, my anachronism. I applied for a credit card and it duly arrived in the mail, complete with instructions on how to use it.

Now I'd always used cheques and never had any trouble keeping track of my financial transactions. You write out a cheque for the amount and fill in the butt and the deal's done and recorded. Not so, I found, with credit cards.

Firstly you have to find out if that particular shop takes that particular credit card, and if they do a complicated and esoteric ritual begins. They drag out a machine about the size of a car radio and then get a four-page booklet with two carbon pages in it. That's six bits of paper; I thought these cards were supposed to simplify things!

For some reason the booklets are never kept where the machine is. They have to hunt around somewhere else for them. The book and your credit card are fitted into the machine and half a horsepower is used to push a slide across them and back again. The book is then removed from the machine and the top page is torn off and screwed up and thrown away. The assistant then writes the date, the item, the price and a few other things on the rest of the book and then gives it to you to sign. (I'd like to point out that by this time I could have given them a cheque and been halfway up the street.) Your signature is then checked against the one on the credit card, and then the yellow page is extracted from the booklet and given to you along with your card. It's enough to put a bloke off shopping.

I tried to get some money out of one of those money-dispensing machines once. I knew instinctively that they

218

couldn't be trusted: this one dragged my card into itself and refused to give it back again. I thought it must have eaten it or something, but a few days later I got it back in the mail, just when I thought I'd seen the last of it.

Within a month of using the credit card my affairs were in a terrible mess. I had no idea how much I'd spent and I had these blasted bits of yellow paper all through my pockets and in the car and round the house. And when I got the bill from the credit card crowd I nearly fell over with shock. It took me weeks to claw my way back from the brink of insolvency.

I still cart that card around, I've found a use for it. I've gone back to using the old cheque book and the card has come in handy for ID, twice in two years.

The biggest gap between me and modern technology, and the thing that convinced me I was born thirty years later than I should have been, was the computer.

"Get yourself a word processor, Crumpy," they said to me. "No one uses those old typewriters any more, they're out of date. You can just write straight onto a word processor and alter the material around any way you like. Then you simply print it out."

Simply print it out? I couldn't help being a bit sceptical about that, but I finally gave in to the pressure and made enquiries about a word processor at a place that supplied them.

"Not a problem, sir," said the young man in a white shirt and blue tie. "I can get you started on one of our IBM personal computers with the Wordperfect package in half an hour."

"Half an hour?"

"Less," he assured me. "These models are so simple a child can use them."

"Okay," I said, not without some trepidation. "I'll give it a go."

The young man in the white shirt and blue tie delivered

the machine himself. It was in four big cardboard boxes. We unpacked it and set it up on the sittingroom table, the only surface in the house big enough to take it all. Then we found that there weren't enough power outlets in the room to plug in all the components, so I had to run an extension lead up the passage from the kids' bedroom and roust out every double-adapter in the house. I took the best part of an hour to get it set up, all hooked together and running.

The computer man seated himself at the keyboard and rubbed his hands together and flexed his fingers like a concert pianist about to play something on the piano.

"Now let's see," he said. "It's a while since I've used the Wordperfect function."

He rattled the keys and symbols, numbers and words began appearing on the screen. The computer man paused and thought for a moment.

"That's not right," he said. "Hang on, I'll just check the menu again."

I didn't like the look of this. If a bloke in a white shirt and blue tie couldn't handle this contraption, how the hell was I going to be able to?

He mucked it up again and decided to consult the instruction book, which was a four-inch thick, two-hundred-page volume, written in some sort of foreign language.

We persevered, and two hours later we had the whole process written down on a piece of paper, each key or keys I had to use for everything from enter to exit, including the print-out function. It worked when we tried it. The young man in the white shirt and blue tie departed in what I thought was rather indecent haste. I think he thought I was a bit thick or something.

That evening I sat myself at the computer, switched her on, pushed the right sequence of keys and in no time at all I was rattling away good-oh. By the time I was ready to knock off I had about three thousand words stashed in the machine. I decided to print it out so I could have something tangible to show for my labours.

I must have done something wrong because the printer wouldn't start printing when I told it to. I turned it off at the wall to clear it so I could start again, and then I couldn't find anything to print. My three thousand words seemed to have disappeared somewhere. In the finish I gave up and went to bed with a grave feeling of disquiet. Three thousand irreplaceable words!

The next morning I rang the young man with the white shirt and blue tie and told him what had happened.

"Didn't you save it?" he said.

"Save what?" I said. "You told me that once it was in there you couldn't lose it."

"Only if you save it," he said.

"Then I've lost it," I said.

"I'm afraid so," he said. "You have to remember to save it."

Save it? If I'd been on a boat just then that infernal machine would have been given a buoyancy-test. And to make matters worse, when I got home that night the kids were squabbling over some games they'd found on the thing. It was as easy as pie to them. They seem to have been born to it. I know I wasn't. Anachronology! Thirty years ahead of my time!

My wife and kids ganged up on me and persuaded me to keep the computer for the kids' education. Leisure Suit Larry? Education?

It sits there still, shrouded in mystery, dominating the sitting room, intimidating me. I could never trust that thing again, I'm too anachronistic, I'd feel much more at home with a pencil and paper or a manual typewriter, only they don't make those any more. They all have to be plugged into the power these days.

BODIES

I'VE BEEN THINKING lately, wondering about things, and I think I've come up with the cause of most of humanity's problems. It's – don't laugh – it's bodies.

We all come into the world in much the same way and on arrival everyone is given a body, and I reckon this body, this subtle combination of the elements, is one of the neatest tricks God plays on us.

Keeping a body going is a full-time, life-long inescapable obligation. For a start, the body has to be constantly supplied with air. When we stop breathing we start dying. That's number one. There's no choice, we breathe or we die.

Then there's food and drink, a perpetual necessity. A huge part of our existence is occupied with eating and drinking. Life depends on it. All the agriculture, horticulture, farming, market-gardening, transportation, refrigeration, preservation and cooking of food. Foremost amongst the industries, every body needs sustenance.

Another responsibility for anyone owning a body is to see that it is kept reasonably clean and tidy. It has to be washed every day, its teeth have to be brushed, its hair has to be kept cut and groomed, its nails have to be clipped and its armpits deodorised. Only then, and dressed in clean clothes, is a body considered fit to go out and mingle with other bodies.

Then, of course, the body has to be kept within a narrow few degrees of temperature. This is where clothing comes into it. Everybody has to wear clothes. None of the animals have to wear clothes, they're born with them, but all people have to wear clothes, and, as if this wasn't enough, God made us susceptible to vanity. The result of this is that society spends a vast proportion of its resources and energy in the production and wearing of clothing, plus all the adornments demanded by the vain. Dyes for hair, colouring for faces, rings for ears and fingers, bones for noses, paint for nails, jewels for the wealthy and fashion for the foolish. And all this clothing has to be kept washed, and that necessitates another huge industry and its offshoots.

As well as clothing there's the myriad of other devices designed to keep bodies within survival temperature. Every house and other building, all the heating and cooling and insulating, everything has to conform to the principle of keeping us cosy, from the igloo in the Arctic to the ceiling fan at the equator.

As well as all that, these flimsy pieces of apparatus we call our bodies have to be protected from injury. There has to be protective clothing, gloves, helmets, boots, pads, shields, even bullet-proof vests. All the handrails, safety harnesses, covers, guards, boundaries, fences, alarms, warnings, lights, education, laws, life-jackets and lectures to help us avoid injury to our bodies. A huge industry, the protection one.

Yet another whopper that was laid on us along with our bodies is the fact that they're prone to a large range of malfunctions. Maladies of all description assail our fragile hold on health, necessitating vast expenditures and effort in all the regions. Health professionals have to be trained, hospitals built and maintained, research centres and sciences established all over the world, because our bodies break down on us now and again.

To make our bodies even trickier to handle we've been given brains, and our bodies are subject to semi-controllable urges that our brains tell us are bad for us. When our bodies win the struggle our brains feel bad about it, and when our brains win out our bodies are frustrated. It's a no-win situation.

You can't just put a body here and leave it to itself, you have to teach it things so it can survive in the environment. It has to be educated. Learning institutions must be erected and staffed and attended and maintained. After attending one or more of these institutions for ten or more years a body is considered qualified to enter the work force as a man or woman, or they might enter into a marriage with another man or woman and bring forth other bodies to keep the process going.

If a body chooses to take up a trade or profession, whatever it is it will be connected in some way with the maintenance of bodies. A craftsman uses his body to make a chair for bodies to sit on. The farmer and the pharmacologist, the sailor and the seamstress, the mahout and the mechanic, the peasant and politician, the tea-lady and tribesman – all are enslaved to the unarguable law that bodies must be maintained and protected at all times above all else.

Throughout the ages mankind has performed wonderful feats of discovery and invention, progressing ever onwards towards more refined methods of nurturing our bodies. Giant strides have been made in the fields of nutrition and medical science. In fact, all science, like every other human activity, is dedicated in some way to the well-being of the body.

You'd think something so important to us and so close to us would have been figured out by this time, but the fact is that we don't even know why we have to go to sleep. We spend a third of our lives asleep and don't even know what for. It might be something as simple as us needing a spell from the constant effort needed to keep a body on the go, but until we find out for sure there must be a fair bit more about these bodies of ours that we don't know yet.

Everybody who lives has to die, and everybody who ever died passed into other realms not knowing why they spent a third of their lives asleep. It makes me sad to think about that. And when we die the undertaker takes over and therein lies another thriving industry devoted to the body. Its disposal. And along with that there's always a ritual to send brother or sister body on his or her way to wherever the inhabitants of bodies go when bodies die. Another mystery, we continually reassure ourselves and each other that when we die we go to a much better place, and yet when someone does turn up their toes we grieve for them. Doesn't make sense to me, that.

Although my meditations on the mystery of the body may have identified the main problem besetting humanity, I still don't feel that I've come up with any answers, except that I think I might have stumbled on a clue to what it must be like in heaven – the same as here, only no bodies.

I wonder what they find to do up there?

No Reference Intended

ONE OF THE things about writing yarns, whether they're true or not, is that you're always looking for suitable names for your characters. If you use people's actual names you can get yourself into all sorts of strife. The search for a name can hold you up no end, so I took to getting my names from the Death Notices in the newspapers. The people who bore those names wouldn't need them any more and if I mixed surnames and christian names and changed them round a bit no one should even be able to notice, but it wasn't that simple.

I was running my finger down the Obituary column in the *New Zealand Herald* one day, looking for a name for a retired seafaring man, when I came across this entry,

Squad. Leader Flght. Lt. Frederick James Forsyth (72) RNZAF (Ret.) flew his final mission at 0300 hours yesterday morning. Survived and sadly missed by his wife Alison and son Stanley. A service will be held etc

There was the name I wanted, and more. I called my retired seafaring man Stan Forsman, and the bane and first love of his life, the matriarchal matron of a retirement home, was called Ailsa. Ailsa enjoyed bossing Stan around, and Stan enjoyed complaining about it. They'd found a level of communication that suited them both.

Ailsa and Stan went through many adventures, got married

and moved into a cottage and nagged and complained contentedly away at each other for years. At the age of 72 Stan turned up his toes, and his obituary in the *Wanganui Chronicle* read,

Capt. Stanley Forsman, (74) R.N. (ret.) slipped his moorings and sailed with the ebb-tide at 0200 hours. Survived and sadly missed by his wife Ailsa. A service will be held in the Seamen's Chapel in Bartam Road at 10pm on Wednesday 14th June.

You couldn't in all fairness say that anyone should be able to recognise anyone else from that, but within a month of its publication I had a letter from a woman telling me she'd recognised her uncle, a bloke called Sam Foster, in my story and she wanted to know anything I could tell her about him. 'He'd apparently become very reticent in his declining years and the family were anxious to find out anything they could about his life from his associates and friends.

This necessitated the writing of a longish letter of denial and explanation, and I'd no sooner got that out of the way than another letter arrived, this time from a bloke who wrote to say that he'd instantly recognised his uncle, his mother's brother, a bloke called Sven Foreman, in the same story. Did I know Sven when he was working in the coal mines or when he was in the Merchant Marine Service on the Tasman run? His relatives in Denmark would appreciate any information they could get about him. Another letter of denial and explanation was required.

Yet another letter informed me that Stan Forsman was a missing relative of the writer and they'd been trying to contact him ever since they'd lost touch with him during the Sydney waterfront strike in seventy-one. Did I have a present address for him? They enclosed a faded photograph of a faceless bloke in a waistcoat and baggy pants. I had to return the photo, it was the only one they had of him, and another letter was required to put the record straight.

No, it doesn't matter what name you use, someone is likely to say it's their uncle, their cousin, their father, their missing relative, a friend of theirs or somebody they know. It doesn't matter how fictional or far-out your character is, there's no guarantee that someone isn't going to think they recognise someone they know from it.

I wrote a book about a bloke called Long Harry Long. His old man, Harry Long, reckoned that Harry was the only name to call a boy and named both his sons Harry. The older Harry was taller than the younger one and became known as Long Harry Long. The younger one was Short Harry Long. To add to the confusion Short Harry Long grew taller than Long Harry Long, so Short Harry was the taller Long boy and Long Harry was the shorter one. To top this off I gave their mother the name of Whatu. And I got a letter from a reader asking if they were any relation to the Longs from Tutukaka.

To try and head this sort of thing off I've made up characters called Esso, Haystack, Fiff, Dollar, Guilty, Whatcher, Ponto, Dodge, Thump and many others. I called one of my characters Diesel and later on I met a bloke who'd read the book and wanted to know where I'd run across his brother, whose name was Diesel. I think he finally believed my explanation that I'd got the name from the side of a truck when I pointed out that my Diesel was a nine-year-old Maori boy and his brother was a thirty-year-old Pakeha.

You can write about Harry Hangloose the surfing bum, Percy Pistonbroke the racing driver, Garry Grubscrew the repair man, Bertie Bungnose the brat, Penelope Prickfinger the dressmaker, Merven Mincemaggot the apprentice chef, Lucy

Lastic the nervous first-year school mistress, or Randy Ribeye the by-jovial butcher. No matter how fantastic your fiction is someone will swear they know the actual person it's taken from, because truth is indeed stranger than fiction.

I wouldn't mind betting that if someone wrote a story about a bloke called Weetbix Phnat who, along with his faithful offsider Garn Withyuh, wins a scholarship and locks himself in a research lab of the Phailem University and investigates the possible beneficence of frog-liver oil as a preventive of hereditary rickets in the female bumble-bee, someone would still write to the author saying that they'd been at school with Weetbix and they'd lost contact with him. Any information as to his present whereabouts would be greatly appreciated.

So if any of the characters in this book remind you of someone you know, please remember the bit at the front that says, "No reference intended. . .". It's fair dinkum. That's my yarn anyway, and I'm stickin' to it.

Song of a Drifter

I've cut me load, and that's me song,
It's time I hit the track,
I've been round here for far too long
And now I'm headin' back.

I'm splittin' from this worn-out scene,
I'm packin' up my gear,
I'm taking off for pastures green,
I'm snatchin' it from here.

I've heard the things they said to me,
I've bogged meself in stuff,
I've took responsibility
And now I've had enough.

I'll drag me hook, I'll just un-front,
I'm headin' for the door,
I'm castin' off, I'll pole me punt,
I'm not here any more.

So good luck, mate, I'm movin' on,
I'll leave the place to you,
And if they ask you where I've gone
Just tell them I shot through.

And if we meet some other place
A stranger you will be,
I can't remember name or face,
They're all the same to me.

I'll greet you like a brother,
I'll make you laugh somehow,
And then one day I'll drift away,
Just like I'm doin' now.